PENGUIN BOOKS

MY FIRST POPSICLE

Zosia Mamet is perhaps best known for her starring role in the Emmy- and Golden Globe Award–winning HBO series *Girls*, and her role in the Emmy-nominated HBO Max series *The Flight Attendant*. When she isn't on-screen, you can find her at the barn riding her horse, or at home in the woods with her husband, snuggling their dog.

MY FIRST POPSICLE

 An Anthology of Food and Feelings

Edited by

Zosia Mamet

PENGUIN BOOKS

PENGUIN BOOKS
An imprint of Penguin Random House LLC
penguinrandomhouse.com

Illustrations by Yan Yu Lee

LIBRARY OF CONGRESS CATALOGING-IN-PUBLICATION DATA
Names: Mamet, Zosia, 1988– editor.
Title: My first popsicle: an anthology of food and feelings / edited by Zosia Mamet.
Description: [New York]: Penguin Books, [2022]
Identifiers: LCCN 2022013126 (print) | LCCN 2022013127 (ebook) |
ISBN 9780143137290 (hardcover) | ISBN 9780593511251 (ebook)
Subjects: LCSH: Cooking. | Food—Psychological aspects. | Dinners and
dining—Psychological aspects. | Celebrities—Social life and customs.
Classification: LCC TX714 .M925 2022 (print) | LCC TX714 (ebook) |
DDC 641.5—dc23/eng/20220726
LC record available at https://lccn.loc.gov/2022013126
LC ebook record available at https://lccn.loc.gov/2022013127

Printed in the United States of America
1st Printing

Set in Meridien LT Pro with Macklin Slab,
Macklin Serif, and La Luxes Serif
Designed by Sabrina Bowers

To everyone who contributed to
and made this book possible

CONTENTS

INTRODUCTION

Zosia Mamet

THERE ARE A FEW THINGS WE CAN'T LIVE WITHOUT. I mean, there are things we *think* we can't live without, like coffee or sex or our favorite television show. But in terms of basic survival, the things we actually need are few in number. Water, oxygen, sleep, and food. And maybe love. But that's if you wanna get existential about it, and I feel like we should stay literal for the time being. So, the first three things are obviously essential. But also slightly boring. Water, oxygen, sleep, sure . . . Food? That's something else entirely. Food as a subject is a black hole. It is a word ripe with associations: stories, attachments, memories, disorders, emotions, hang-ups . . . the list is endless. My point being that at the end of the day we all have thoughts and feelings and emotions when it comes to food, certain foods more than others. But all of us, just the same. And given that food is listed as one of the few basic things we need to survive, I think we often forget how intimate our connections are to this topic. So I wanted to create a book of stories that highlighted that connection.

This all started a few years ago when my husband, Evan, and I went out to dinner with two friends of ours. During the meal, the wife took out her phone and said that she had to show us the cutest video. It was of their two-year-old son having a popsicle for the first time. The video was incredible. In the video, his mom hands him the popsicle and he tentatively puts it to his lips. He immediately pulls the popsicle away and starts to cry, but then a wave of curiosity washes over his face and he *very* slowly touches the popsicle to his lips again. There are another few moments where he looks slightly confused and is certainly debating the pros and cons of whether to venture forward or abandon the mission of this cold, sweet, alien thing. But eventually he takes the plunge and shoves the popsicle in his mouth. And then . . . the most epically massive smile breaks out over his face, and he starts to cackle in an infectiously giddy way. So the broken-down *TV Guide* version of this two-minute iPhone video is: kid eats popsicle for the first time. Sounds pretty mundane, right? But believe me when I tell you that this video was striking on so many levels. I hadn't thought about experiencing a food for the first time in . . . I couldn't even re-member. Let alone having *actually* experienced a new food for the first time. Probably not since I was around this boy's age. And the range of emotions that played across his face throughout this short video was exceptional. It was like watching a brilliant French mime. He hit all the big ones: fear, confusion, dislike, distaste, sadness, joy, jubilation. It was all there. And it was *new*. He had discovered something. I was blown away by it. And I couldn't stop thinking about it. As we walked home from dinner, it was as if a burr had gotten stuck in my brain, scratching away at it. *Food and emotions . . . food and emotions . . .* the three words kept knocking about in my head like a pinball machine.

And then, over the next few days or weeks (I'm not entirely sure of the timeline here; my memory isn't great), the topic continued to stew. I suffered from severe anorexia growing up, so I have my own history and emotionally fraught connection to food. I thought deeply about that on a personal level: my journey with it; the stories I had to tell about food, in general; specific foods, dishes, and my feelings toward them. And then, as I thought more about it, I realized how universal this topic is. No matter who you are, what your upbringing was, where you came from, your religion, your age, your profession, *no matter what*, we all have some form of emotional connection to food and stories to tell about it.

Once the idea had fully formed in my brain, I became convinced that this had to have been done before. Somebody had for sure already written this book. I knew I wanted it to be an anthology. I wanted to acquire as many essays from as many wonderfully different human beings as I could and hear *their* stories about food. I had a few to tell, but who wants to hear only from me? So I reached out to my book agents and I told them the idea. And they too thought, "This is potentially a good idea—it has to have been done before." They did their due diligence and some deep digging to see if anything like this book existed. And hark! It did not! So in a conference room at Janklow & Nesbit on a very hot Manhattan afternoon, *My First Popsicle* was born.

I wrote up a little pitch/prompt to send to folks to get the creative juices flowing (please note that I will insert as many awful dad-joke food puns into this introduction as possible, so sorry not sorry). And I decided to start by dipping my toe in, or, I guess you could say, dipping my finger into the sauce? That one doesn't quite work. Anyway, I sent it to a few friends and asked if this book was something that they might consider writing a piece for. And every person came back with a resounding yes. Then I asked two friends whom I love and admire as writers. I knew I wanted the book to be comprised of some essays by professional writers, but also by humans from all walks of life, artists of all different kinds—some cooks, musicians, actors, singers—really, whoever had an interesting story to tell and would say yes to writing an essay. But I thought it wise to ask two writers first. So I did. My prompt was very loose because I wanted to give the contributors the longest leash possible and the fewest parameters to hopefully allow them to write whatever they wanted without confines. Basically, my criterion was: it needs to be about food and feelings, go. What I got back were two of the most beautiful essays I have ever read. And they were exactly what I had hoped for. Both were about food (one more than the other) and an emotional, circumstantial connection to that food or dish. And they were both wonderful, engaging, and personal stories deeply specific to the humans who had written them. And they were both *vastly* different. I was over the fucking moon.

And then, I got a job. My day job—acting. So that took up a bunch of time. And then a global pandemic happened, and the world shut down. And then, I don't know, my brain broke? And for some reason, *My First Popsicle* got put in a drawer in the back of my mind. Until one chilly morning in January, Evan and I were having coffee in our kitchen in upstate New York, and out of nowhere he said, "Whatever happened with the cookbook?" And I didn't really have a good response. I sat there and thought about it for a moment, and all I could say was, "I don't know. It just kind of got put on pause." And he said, "That was a great idea, you should pick it up again." And so I did.

I'm sort of like a dog with a bone. When my brain hooks on, or in this case hooks back on, to an idea, I *go*. So I wrote to my book agents and told them I was picking *Popsicle* back up, and off I went. Full steam ahead. I shot off emails like a chipmunk on Adderall. My agents had told me that with the two essays we already had, we'd probably want a list of ten confirmed contributors to go out and pitch the book with and a list of about twenty more that I would reach out to once we had a buyer. It took me a week. The responses to my "Hey, here's this idea I have for a cookbook/book of essays. Wanna write a piece for it?" emails were swift in coming, and short of someone writing their own book, just having a baby, or shooting an epic film in Serbia, the responses were always a deeply excited *yes*. And that sealed the deal for me. These human beings who I loved and admired and revered were excited to write about this topic for my book. It felt surreal. I felt like our friend's toddler experiencing the joy of his first popsicle.

I am still pinching myself that this book, this potluck of words from all of these exceptionally special literary cooks, has come together. I am so grateful to each and every one of them for sharing their histories and stories and thoughts and feelings about food for this book. Some of these stories are raw and gut-wrenching. Some are make-your-face-hurt funny. But they are all personal and from the heart. And isn't that when food tastes best? When it's made with love?

I hope you enjoy reading this book as much as I have enjoyed creating it. May you relish in the words, make delicious messes attempting to cook the recipes, and feast on the beautiful images. Bon appétit.

Made with love,

CONTENT NOTE

HELLO, READER! THANK YOU FOR EMBARKING ON THIS literary/culinary adventure with us. We hope you enjoy every page of this book as much as we all enjoyed creating it for you.

I wanted to give you a heads-up before you venture further into these pages. I gave the contributors free rein to write about whatever they wanted as long as, at its core, their essays came back to food and feelings. Some chose to write silly essays or comedic ones or light-hearted stories. But there are also essays within the pages of this book that deal with some heavy matters.

The goal behind this book was to show that our relationship to food is varied and complicated and can span myriad emotions, and sometimes those emotions lead us to dark places. These essays are just as beautiful and important as the others, but I wanted you, reader, to know that they live here, in case the subject matter is triggering for you. There are essays that deal with the topics of disordered eating, absent parents, death, dysfunctional families, insecurity, loneliness, self-hatred. I am not warning you about these essays so you don't read them, but just so you know they're there.

I would also add that I feel honored to have these pieces in the book because these are all, sadly, common issues that so many of us struggle with. Life is not perfect and it can be incredibly hard. There is no shame in having troubles or struggling. As our contributors show so beautifully in their essays, we all have something. And as someone who has struggled with many things herself—disordered eating, anxiety, depression—I encourage anyone who feels the need to seek help. Lean on those around you, reach out, use the endless resources out there. There is no shame in needing help with whatever it is you may be struggling with. And please always know, you are not alone.

MY FIRST
POPSICLE

POOR MAN'S CAKE

Patti Smith

M Y MOTHER HAD A WAY OF ALWAYS MAKING THINGS better. If my father was on strike at the factory and things looked exceptionally bleak, she would sing show tunes and let my siblings and me stay up late to watch monster movies on our little black-and-white TV. If the refrigerator was nearly empty, she would sit in the kitchen smoking a cigarette, thinking about how to brighten our situation. Then she would get up, flip through her recipe book, and somehow conjure the ingredients for Poor Man's Cake, our favorite hard-times fare.

While we waited for the cake to cool, she would tell us stories of the Great Depression. She told of how families would cross the country in search of work, and how they'd pool their meager supplies and make the same cakes and wrap them in their bandannas, to be assured of something to eat in the morning.

Sometimes she would be obliged to send us off to school with nothing but a chunk of the cake, but that was fine with us. I'd tie up my chunk, a little burned around the edges with lots of raisins, in one of my father's old blue paisley bandannas and imagine I was going west.

We always wondered why it was called Poor Man's Cake. Then after my mother passed away, my sister Linda found two coffee-stained copies of the recipe. She noticed the words NO EGGS at the top of one, solving the riddle. No eggs or milk, both expensive back then, were required. Just simple ingredients, stirred with a wooden spoon and poured into a cast-iron loaf pan.

Recently, Linda made me my own Poor Man's Cake. Breaking off a chunk, I pictured my mother in her housecoat, inevitably spattered with batter, sitting at the kitchen table pouring a cup of coffee. Linda's cake, made with our mother's recipe, brought back the happiest memories of the one who always found a way to laugh away tears and feed us when we were hungry.

Poor Man's Cake

NO EGGS

INGREDIENTS:

2 cups sugar
2 cups raisins
2 cups water
1 cup margarine
Pinch of salt
2 teaspoons ground cloves
2 teaspoons cinnamon
3½ cups sifted all-purpose flour

Preheat the oven to 350°F.

Grease and flour a 9 x 13-inch baking dish

Place all the ingredients, aside from the flour, in a large saucepan on top of the stove.

Bring to a boil and stir.

Set aside to cool.

When cool, add the flour, stirring it in with a wooden spoon.

Pour the mixture into a greased and floured 9 × 13-inch baking dish.

Bake for about 1 hour or until a toothpick comes out clean when inserted in the middle.

SHALLOT VINAIGRETTE INSURANCE

 Stephanie Danler

T HE NEW YORK CITY BOXES CAME ON A MOVING TRUCK
to the cottage in Laurel Canyon. Pomelo trees scraped the
roof of the truck when it turned in, so it couldn't pull all the
way into the long drive. I helped two guys from the moving company
carry my stuff the rest of the way up to a shed. These boxes had been
in a storage unit in the Brooklyn Navy Yard for three years, since my
divorce. I felt like I had been much younger when I packed them.

The first box I opened had sweaters in it. His and mine. I remember
taping up that box and thinking that we would be right back. That we
were separating, dismantling our home in a cold spring, but we would
be unpacking this box before the next snow came. Surveying my things
in the shed, I looked at my KitchenAid stand mixer, halfheartedly protected by plastic wrap gone loose. A box of antique Bundt pans, collected at flea markets. I opened another box that had KITCHEN written

on the side. It was full of Mason jars. Or what had been Mason jars. They were pulverized glass at this point. It hurt afresh to see it all again. To remember my ex-husband and me circling the tiny Williamsburg apartment, packing it all up, drinking iced coffee after iced coffee, not knowing how to speak to each other. I still loved him. He still loved me. We wept constantly, without ceremony, in front of the movers. They avoided us, whispering to each other in Polish. Surely, we would be coming right back to each other. It wasn't possible that there had been many snows since then, snowstorms when I hadn't even thought of him, or that I had moved to a place unmarked by that kind of weather.

Beyond books, most of these boxes were part of a kitchen. My marriage had revolved around food and wine. Our lives were spent in our respective restaurants where we worked the requisite twelve-hour days, and our leisure time was spent in the restaurants of our friends. I opened another box and there was my ex-husband's bourbon collection. I laughed. Rare releases of Blanton's and WhistlePig rye, even a bottle of Pappy Van Winkle I had scavenged for his birthday. The storage unit where they'd been residing was not climate controlled. Was the whiskey still drinkable? Yes, we had packed them like idiots full of denial. How much of our lives had we wasted in that way?

For the seven years of our relationship we were what Laurie Colwin calls "domestic sensualists." We never ate for subsistence, only for experience. We entertained frequently and ambitiously. We made cassoulet from scratch, including grinding the meat and stuffing the sausage casings. It took weeks. Pastas were kneaded, rolled, and cut; cheeses were tempered under mesh domes; slivers of truffles were slid under the skin of capons. We had a culinary book collection with rare cookbooks from Kitchen Arts & Letters and Bonnie Slotnick. My ex-husband brewed beer, and each season we pickled, dropping the Mason jars into boiling water. Jars of ramps, onions, and cucumbers lined up, throwing colored light. We changed glassware as we revolved our wines, moving from stemless aperitif-style glasses to slim white-wine glasses to Burgundy bowls. After dinner we often moved the dining table to the side of the room so we could dance.

This decadence occurred in accordance with the full blooming of a zeitgeist, my ex-husband and I riding a wave that surfaced after the millennium with Anthony Bourdain, April Bloomfield, and David Chang, but one that had broken in the mid-aughts and—joyfully—kept breaking. Restaurants were New York City's cutthroat sport. It seemed everyone was discovering the Jura wine region in France, or the salinity of Manzanilla sherry, or the pucker of fish sauce. That our passions were considered niche (at best) to the rest of the world didn't bother us. In the city, we spoke the same language of taste. Every discretionary penny was thrown into this search for pleasure. My discovery of the food world coincided with my marriage and became inseparable. That made it seem less like a graciously prolonged moment and more like the banquet that would always be my life.

When I left our apartment in Williamsburg—and it was my first home, really—I moved into a room in a Victorian town house in Bushwick. I had only a mattress, books, and a dining table as a desk. Two suitcases of clothes. The rest of it I locked away in the storage unit. Eight other people lived in this house. I rarely saw them or even heard them.

Regardless of the weather, my room had the powdery gray light of a storybook orphanage. I wore sandals in the shower. I could play music in my room only at certain hours. It was impossible not to feel that I had left a vibrant adulthood for an ashen version of myself at twenty-two: broke, prickly with loneliness. No belongings, no footing. The kitchen in this formerly grand town house was a playground for mice and cockroaches. Only one of the roommates ever used it. He was an Indian man, a photographer in his late forties, and he made his own Indian food every evening. The scent dominated the hallways. I could smell that his ghee was rancid, and I always wanted to say something, but I was ashamed of my snobbery. One morning there was mice shit in a line across the bottom of my bed. I didn't trust my own authority on anything.

I stopped enjoying food. Wine felt flabby and desperate without the accompaniment. The act of changing out stemware (in an apartment with no dishwasher!) came to stand in for the fraudulence of my married life. I had become a bourgeois mannequin, had taken to caring about the wrong things. Alone again, I was safest when caring about nothing. Take-out containers piled up inside my room until I got nervous that the kitchen mice would find them. Tuna salad from a bodega, eaten with Triscuits; jars of cornichons; Greek yogurt; round after round of toast. Fried rice and steamed vegetables I could get from a Chinese place for less than ten dollars, which I could make last a week. It wasn't just that my financial situation had drastically changed; I knew well from married life that a vat of Marcella Hazan's minestrone could be half eaten, the other half frozen, and would be gratifying on both occasions. Cooking is nearly always the cheaper option. Yet I did not cook in that house for a year. Not even an egg. It was a form of self-recrimination. Even the thought of these once-sacred rituals made me feel empty. I had stopped believing in their power.

Depression is always a taste to me. The tongue desiccated and parched, the oversteeped and forgotten tea, the tilting-toward-decay fizziness of sour grapes. An ambient and unspecific sense of death that keeps you from your senses. I lost food and accepted it. Though I quit cooking, I still walked to the Union Square Greenmarket in all seasons. Out of habit, I still checked out Lani's Farm, Guy Jones, Keith's, and still waved to the farmers I knew. On an unremarkable winter day I bought a shallot.

A smooth, lavender teardrop of a shallot.

It was a joke among my college friends that I couldn't boil water for pasta. Maybe it was because my mother was a gifted cook who had gone to culinary school, or because we were estranged and I imagined myself nothing like her, or because I had been working in restaurants since I was fifteen years old—but I came into my twenties completely dependent on others to feed me. That changed when I moved to New York City and started serving at Union Square Cafe. But I didn't teach myself to cook because I was inspired. I did it because I fell in love. I had just started dating my future husband and we were planning a trip to Paris. We had a lengthy list of restaurants to hit, but we had rented an apartment with the idea that we would also go to the markets and cook at home. The fact that neither one of us cooked did not impede this fantasy. I assumed that my general knowledge of food would translate into a virtuoso performance in the kitchen. I assumed that by buying myself *The Art of Simple Food* by Alice Waters, reading it cover to cover, carting it over to Paris, I would, in a small but significant way, become Alice Waters vacationing in Paris with her love. The culinary results of that Paris trip were edible but not close to transcendent. I remember reading that I should skim the fat off a beef stew and not understanding the direction. Instead I stirred as hard as I could so that fat stopped collecting on the top. I kept burying it. That, to me, was skimmed.

But one of the simpler recipes I did manage to execute in Paris was a shallot vinaigrette. While the vinaigrette came out just good enough the first time (there was too much acid to oil, but I was interested exclusively in sharp flavors back then), it was still exciting: Why would anyone buy salad dressing if they could make this? In the years to come I always had a jar of it in the fridge. It went on lettuces, on rice and farro, on steamed kale, on baked potatoes and omelets, on one hundred avocados.

In addition to a finely chopped shallot, the recipe calls for vinegar and oil. Though I prefer red wine or sherry, whatever vinegar is on hand is probably fine. I've also been known to add, according to mood and availability: lemon zest, anchovies, fresh thyme, chopped soft herbs like parsley or chives, fish sauce, Aleppo pepper, crème fraîche. The key to the recipe—which isn't really a recipe as much as a gesture—is time. That means maceration. Leave the shallots and the acid alone together for an hour. The shallots will flush and plump. They will lose their rawness to the vinegar. They become their own element, not simply an accompaniment.

Shallot vinaigrette was the first thing I made in my transient Bushwick kitchen. It needed something to be spooned over. And so I made something to spoon it over. It did not feel like an achievement. It felt like eating, an urge temporarily satiated. But seeing the leftovers in a jar in the fridge begged me to make something else. I bought eggs and butter. I bought the good sourdough and the leftover ends of expensive cheeses: gouda, comté, triple crèmes. Dried lentils. Cans of cannellini beans, rinsed, splashed with olive oil, just heated through. I bought a head of Little Gem lettuce and a watermelon radish. Because I had the radish and the vinegar, why not do a quick pickle of it? It wasn't exactly a triumph over dark forces: the symphony swelling, me throwing back the heavy drapes to face the sunlight. But this is how I started over. I did not have my own plates or mugs; I had my own jar of vinaigrette.

Standing in the Laurel Canyon shed with my mangled boxes, just about as far as I could get from Brooklyn, I had so much sympathy for the idiots who packed them. That sympathy made it impossible to separate my life into organized compartments—my phases, my lovers, my sublets. I don't believe anymore that I was one person in my marriage and another when it was over, that those selves were disparate and unrepeatable. The halcyon meals of the marriage, its disappearance, and leaving New York City—it was all a wash of loss and creation. The truth is that even within that frenzy of epicurean highs, there were the seeds of our collapse. There was our penchant for drinking too much, our delirious avoidance of conflict, my fear of vulnerability, and my lust for all sorts of lives outside of matrimony. It was—much like the present moment—both paradisaical and cautionary. "The good news," a friend said to me, "is that you did it once. You know you can do it again." She meant making a home, but of course when it landed on me, it was about love. I do not live in Williamsburg or Bushwick or even Laurel Canyon anymore, but there are things from my first marriage that I've carried with me and have no idea what to do with. But I did cook again. I unpacked the kitchen boxes and started calling those things *mine* instead of *ours*. New beliefs emerged: A shallot vinaigrette in the fridge is insurance against hunger. There is nothing more elegant than eating leftovers with your hands. Time is the key element of any recipe. I am still learning how to skim the fat.

Shallot Vinaigrette

Finely dice some shallots.

Cover with vinegar (I prefer red wine or sherry).

Sprinkle some salt.

Leave to macerate for an hour or up to overnight.

Come back and add good olive oil (the traditional ratio is three parts oil to one part vinegar, but I usually do this to taste).

Optional: black pepper, Aleppo pepper, lemon zest, anchovies (let them macerate as well—they'll break down), fresh thyme, chopped soft herbs like parsley or chives, fish sauce, crème fraîche.

SUMMERTIME ON LONG ISLAND

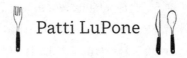

Patti LuPone

I'M LONG ISLAND BORN AND BRED. I EAT SHELLFISH, I YEARN for it, I never turn it down on a menu. Every time I see steamers, or pissers, as we call them, on a menu, I order them. I had a basketful in Maine recently and they were good, but the best ones come from my beloved Northport Bay.

They say you can take the kid out of Northport Bay and Long Island Sound, but you can't take the bay waters and all its succulent treasures out of the kid.

As children, we'd wait for low tide—that distinct, overpowering scent of life and death, muddy waters with creatures just below the surface but at the shoreline—ah!

Steamers, littlenecks, cherrystones, mussels, all for the scraping and picking.

Once, I ate a bushelful of raw littlenecks. Had my knife, pried the delectables open, and scarfed the clams down.

My dad belonged to the Kiwanis Club, and they would have clam-bakes at Crab Meadow Beach. I will always treasure the memory of those days and nights: the deep hole, dug in the early morning; the fire and coals; the seaweed; the crustaceans, the corn, and the potatoes all steamed to perfection; and we still hunted at the water's edge because it was fun!

Any crab, shrimp, clam, or lobster takes me home to summertime on Long Island.

Russell's
Linguine con Vongole

30 littleneck clams

Scrub the outside of the shells, then put the clams into a bowl filled with cold water and lots of salt to clean the sand out, and put the bowl in the fridge for a few hours.

IN PREPARATION TO COOK:

Place into a large sauté pan (with a cover):

Olive oil—enough to cover about half the pan
Anchovy paste—about a 3-inch length of paste from the tube
Red pepper flakes—about 1 teaspoon
Fresh garlic—6 large cloves, thinly sliced

WHEN READY TO COOK:

Turn on heat to medium under the pan, then stir until all the ingredients meld together and become fragrant.

Add clams and cover.

Check after about 5 minutes, shaking the pan back and forth a bit to help the clams open.

Once the clams are all open, remove from the heat—it's done.

Pour over buttered linguine cooked al dente.

Sprinkle with finely chopped fresh Italian parsley.

Salt to taste, if needed!

Toss and enjoy!

BALL BUSTER

 Andrew Bevan

H OW WAS I MEANT TO KNOW THAT THE MOMENT I took a giant bite of that meatball, my entire world would crash down?

It was a midweek Valentine's Day evening. I was in my midtwenties. My boyfriend and I sat at an intimate, cash-only Italian boîte called Max on Avenue B and East Fourth Street, a place the *Times* had rubberstamped as serving well-prepared food with warmth. It was the perfect low-key, low-pressure, unpretentious, romantic neighborhood spot to celebrate a low-key, low-pressure, unpretentious, romantic relationship. After years of chasing the proverbial golden ring of trendy New York hotspots and the aloof throngs of cool urbanites that inhabited them, tonight felt comforting and beautifully habitual.

I had a history of throwing myself at dudes where the only prerequisites were that they occasionally held a guitar or a skateboard and were as unemployed as they were emotionally unavailable. Set up by my coworker three years prior, this was the sanest and sincerest partnership

I'd ever experienced. As a whole, it felt like a significant change of habit from the flash-in-the-pan novelty of my past dalliances. My first blissfully regular, real, and reliable adult union. While my boyfriend did exhibit the ideal mussed brown locks of a skater dude, he called and showed up when he said he would. He was polite, measured, contemplative, and complimentary. He loved his family and had good but not stuffy taste. I was seduced by his functionality and the functionality of this relationship.

There was an old charm and coziness to the restaurant with its reclaimed wood and Edison bulb accents that were light-years ahead of this now particularly ubiquitous Mumford & Sons design crutch. My boyfriend and I sat across from each other, tightly flanked by two straight couples. On my left was an older turtlenecked married pair who looked like they were in a high-end optical ad. On my right was an overly touchy thirtysomething duo. She clutched a bodega bouquet of two dozen roses with baby's breath. They were clearly just hitting their three-month mark.

New Yorkers must develop tunnel vision when dining at the city's many cramped restaurants, lest the chatter, compelling (good and bad) sartorial choices, or PDA of our table neighbors prove too distracting. Worse is the accidental eye contact that leads to a perfunctory "How are the mussels?"—breaking the fourth wall to the point of no return. Your two-top is now a four-top and you're on a double date with strangers. The next thing you know, you're looking at pictures of their three-legged schnauzer and debating whether long-sleeved wedding dresses are evergreen.

As a friendly gay man, whether I'm feeling chatty or not, I somehow either instigate or attract these impromptu conversations. It's a blessing and a curse: it's part of what makes this town *and* being a friendly gay man so great. Yet at times it's essential to keep things one-on-one—especially when your partner is shy and slightly socially awkward, as my boyfriend was.

That Valentine's Day, we were hyperfocused on not breaking the imaginary barrier while we ate our beet and burrata salad with pistachio vinaigrette and toasted garlic bread topped with anchovies—the latter of which he flicked onto my plate before taking a bite. He liked anchovies but knew I loved them more.

We talked about a movie we wanted to see and how his photo shoot that day had ended early instead of late, which never happens. Despite working under one of the best fashion photographers of our time and having his own successful solo career, he had an almost sheepish schoolboy charisma. A year or so before we met, he had lost forty pounds and was now certifiably hot—and it was the holy grail of hot because he didn't love himself enough yet to be narcissistic or egomaniacal. He was a genuinely great guy with a great head of hair (predating the man-bun mania-turned-punch-line), a great heart, and a great career. With him, there was no smoke and mirrors and no gimmicks. He was husband material, the type of man I wanted to marry and then argue with about banal things like him forgetting to buy toothpaste at the store (or, *worse*, buying the expensive, natural, clay-tasting herbal kind) and be secretly annoyed but charmed that he always said "What's doing?" instead of "What's up?"

Our overzealous waiter set down my entrée—a heaping bed of spaghetti covered by a blanket of marinara and topped with extra-large meatballs—with a certain over-Coca-Cola'd (or more likely, cocained) franticness. He seemed desperate for me to take it off his hands. I was happy to oblige.

As a big-city transplant from Colorado, comfort food always seems to take on a lot of meaning. I once dated a twenty-six-year-old who invited me over to his apartment for the first time for dinner and a movie. "His apartment" ended up being his childhood home, and his nanny served us her famous homemade tomato soup and grilled cheese as we watched *The Ring*. With each bite, my shock and awe for a grown-ass man still shamelessly relying on his nanny for supper melted into a euphoric sense of nostalgia and adolescence.

Having the latest food trends and an encyclopedia of far-flung cuisines at our fingertips at any given time (Sri Lankan food at one a.m., quail egg and sea urchin as menu mainstays, waffles sold out of trucks) is part of what sets Manhattan apart. But sometimes you just need something ordinary and straightforward, like spaghetti and meatballs, to amplify your peaks and console your valleys. The culinary equivalent of watching *When Harry Met Sally* for the twenty-eighth time, comfort food grounds you in your happy place, returning you to a simpler, wholesome time, if even just for a moment—a hug in a bite.

"How's the gnocchi?" I asked my boyfriend as I confidently tornado-twisted the pasta onto my fork. I halved one of the enormous meat spheres and popped it into my mouth, a move that was both plucky and presumptuous. I noticed him becoming nervous and visibly shifty, like that kid in the spelling-bee finals too old to be wearing overalls. *The gnocchi must be too dry or the Gorgonzola too strong*, I thought. *Maybe I should give him some of mine.*

He swigged some water, and then . . . he said . . . *it.*

"I don't think I can be in a relationship right now," he muttered in the casual tone usually reserved for commentary like "I don't know if it's going to be cold enough to wear my new coat tomorrow" or "I wonder if the tiramisu here is homemade or frozen." (For the record, I'd order it either way. Any tiramisu is better than no tiramisu.)

So there we sat, wading in our own existential reduction sauce. Was this unrehearsed or premeditated? Trapped on a rustic banquette (in an act of passive-aggressive chivalry, I always offer my dining companion the booth side of the table and then resent them for accepting the gesture), he avoided eye contact. How could he lull me to this place with this sense of homey security only to drop a bomb? A place where the stakes felt so low only a few moments ago. This is not where you break up with someone. This isn't even where you have business discussions or talk about a family will (and even if it were, might I remind you again that it's fucking Valentine's Day). This is a place where the menu is written on chalkboards and they pour molten cheese on top of juicy, sweaty meat orbs. The upcycled and lived-in wooden school chair beneath me and the lone antique lightbulb that swayed ever so slightly above lost their quaintness and suddenly felt hard and cold— fit for a time-out corner or a cinder-block *Law & Order* interrogation room.

I wanted to say "Fuck you, you just gave me your anchovies, you little bitch!" but instead I stared in disbelief with a mouth full of a gargantuan ball of meat. I demanded some sort of eye contact, but his pupils were playing a nervous game of *Frogger*. Curiously, his kind eyes had not instantly turned to dead pools of ink.

Despite being a shamelessly reactionary and emotional person, when the bottom is truly pulled out from under me, I become stupefied and confounded to the point of paralytic shock. The little red string connectors and microchips in my brain seem to melt into a pudding. I freeze, waiting for someone to hit my reset button.

Once I deciphered that what he was saying was actually what he was saying, I realized I essentially had two options:

1. Immediately spit out the ball in a napkin or, better yet, on his face. How great that meat-and-tomato bloodshed would be with ball guts dripping down his puppy-dog cheeks and onto his gray boiled cashmere sweater.

2. Masticate the colossal mass of red meat to completion, which would lead to, I'd say, an awkward pause of about thirteen to sixteen seconds. Ample time for me to gain sustenance for battle.

The meatball was delicious and really the only thing working in my favor at this traumatic moment in my life, despite the fact that it now seemed entirely too inelegant and vulnerable to eat during what was becoming "the last supper." My keen foresight also told me I probably would be too scarred in the future to ever return to this now-tainted establishment, let alone consume a meatball again. There could be some sort of sense memory reminder of him and this night anytime I encountered one for the rest of my life. I did not want to be left with meatball PTSD in perpetuity. I love meatballs. I mean, I *really* love meatballs. So I decided to take the bold step of savoring the bite for a full NINETEEN seconds.

I made a conscious effort to deeply relish that meatball as if it were my death-row meal, taking any solace I suddenly had left in this world from the savory consolation prize of marinara and meat in my mouth. He stared timidly at his plate while strategically moving his food around it. Maybe he was thinking how he'd just ruined gnocchi for himself for years to come. Regardless, he still looked like that spelling-bee kid, but one who was getting scolded by his helicopter parents for accidentally mumbling a swear word after misspelling *eudaemonic* in the final round. Like the time I was sent to the principal's office for yelling "FUCK LIKE A DUCK" after losing a fourth-grade field-day race.

I finished my last chew and swallowed gingerly with an almost ladylike finesse. This was obviously to offset the giant, unapologetic bite I had been working on, or rather, through.

Truth be told, I have a history of biting off more than I can chew, figuratively and quite literally. I'm not a delicate eater, which makes me often fit right in at a Denver barbecue but stick out at the Condé Nast cafeteria or, say, um, a Met Gala or a Chanel dinner. That's not to say I like a mess. I practically came out of the womb in a complete Ralph Lauren look and extra-stiff Bass saddle shoes, and I've always made my bed every day. And though I *love* kids, I often wince at sticky babies drenched in chocolate ice cream or tomato sauce while others continue to assure me how utterly adorable they are.

I've been told since I was probably seventeen that I resemble Ira Glass or Stephen Fry. Though I can now respect both men and also my own face, they're not ideal aesthetic comparisons you want to hear as a teenager starting to creep out of the closet. I've always had a long face, a commanding forehead (that I aptly cover with bangs), a strong chin, two sleepy, contemplative little eyes, and a slight, almost Bernadette Peters–like pout (despite always yearning for a sizable Calista Flockhart or Julia Roberts trap).

While my giant glasses and overly astute visual awareness always seem to compensate for my beady eyes, in what could be some sort of rebellion for the total circumference of my mug or lack thereof, I'm never afraid of having a big mouth of opinions. I am known to take way too big bites in an "I'll show *you* who has a small mouth" kind of way. Who I am trying to prove that to is anyone's guess. As someone who is a nonpicky and very much adventurous eater (to even an annoying degree), I tend to get extra excited about mealtime and food. The delicate chomps go to the wayside. Since I was a kid, I eat my *actual* death-row meal of choice, the cheeseburger, with so much gusto and excitement, it causes me to have these wild, spontaneous hamburger hiccups. I still get them every time, like clockwork.

But that Valentine's Day, I didn't use my extended chewing time wisely and had yet to come up with the perfect clapback or Hail Mary. Once I swallowed, I quickly drained my red-wine glass and said the only clear, logical thing that came to mind:

"Huh?"

"Listen, I don't really want to break up . . . but I just don't think I can be in a relationship either," he said, still refusing to look me in the eye.

"Well, you kind of have to choose, don't you think?" I said with an odd and speedy, almost Bette Davis cadence. It was some kind of weird 1940s fast-talking-dame defense mechanism that appeared out of the blue. I gulped more wine, then skewered and popped another half of a giant orb into my mouth, attacking it a bit more aggressively this time.

At that point, he spouted out some long-winded and neurotic soliloquy of verbal diarrhea that my pudding brain still could not compute. I heard nothing he was saying. I was suddenly Charlie Brown and he was my teacher just spouting out a lot of indecipherable "wah wah woh wah wahs." My focus instead was everywhere else.

I glanced at the three-month couple next to us who were caressing each other's hands. He had just given her a new bracelet. It looked like it would probably turn her wrist green, but, admittedly, it was kind of cute. She batted her fluttery fake eyelashes in slow motion. I hadn't noticed until now how much they looked a lot like little clumps of spiders having a sort of mini standoff with one another on the ends of her eyelids.

The older couple sat silently, sipping some sort of Amaro or Sambuca out of dainty little cordial glasses. I could smell an ominous faint essence of black licorice. I accidentally made eye contact with the woman and caught a glimmer of compassion through her chunky art adviser–looking deep-emerald frames. Or was it commiseration? Maybe she was bracing herself for her own inevitable heartbreak in the near future. Either way, she was eavesdropping, and my eyes darted to the busboy making a quick cameo as he refilled our water glasses. He had more than a few hairs growing from the top of his nose. *Is that even possible?* I thought. I then noticed the droplets from my water glass on the old-time table. It resembled a Jackson Pollock painting. It looked like part of some junior high art teacher's "Life Imitating Art" slideshow.

I kept swirling and chomping and chomping and swirling the moist and tender meat mixture around in my mouth. My mind began to spiral with things like *What am I going to wear tomorrow? Shit. I forgot to pick up my dry cleaning! Are you there, God? It's me, Andrew. I really don't think*

I like Shakespeare. Am I the only one? Has anyone said that out loud? I'm not too fond of iambic pentameter. I like Chekhov—does that count for anything? Should I dye my hair? Yes, these meatballs are very tasty!

I thought of the best Valentine's Day I ever had. Once when I was around eight, my mom threw a really fancy Valentine's Day dinner for me and my brothers and all the kids in the neighborhood. She made a fake restaurant in our house. We dressed up and ate shrimp cocktail and Cornish game hens, pretending we were adults in our little blazers and puffy lace dresses.

I then watched as my boyfriend's lips moved and noticed how relaxed his face was even though his body seemed terribly tense. *Is he really breaking up with me on Valentine's Day?* I thought. *God, he has perfect eyebrows.*

Maybe I would wake up at any moment, and we would laugh about this over spinach-and-egg-white omelets in bed. Or perhaps this would just be something fun we'd tell our grandchildren about someday when we made a fake Valentine's Day restaurant for them (serving spaghetti and meatballs instead of hen). "Grandpa, will you tell us that funny story again when you broke up with Grandpa on Valentine's Day?" they would ask in delight, even though they've heard it twelve times. "Remember, you thought it was over, but it wasn't over because you realized you were truly, deeply, and madly in love with the man, and you made a huge, incredible mistake?"

Over the years, the story would be embellished and become family folklore. Like, that I actually choked on the meatball after "Grandpa" almost broke my heart and he saved my life performing the Heimlich maneuver. When he dislodged the ball, he looked at me, wiped the beef remnants off my face with the sleeve of his gray boiled cashmere sweater, and knew that I was still the one! (The grandkids would love this story.)

I came back to reality just in time to hear him spout a chorus of clichéd and emotionless statements like ". . . which is why I feel like taking a break is the best thing for us." For us? For *us*? Is he saying this is *best* for *me*?

These are the kinds of wallops you expect in breakup texts after a few misguided Tinder dates—not years of spooning, knowing someone's coffee order and the astrological star pattern of moles on their back.

To drive it home, no good breakup is complete without the tried, and often not true, *It's not you; it's me.* "I swear," he pleaded, followed by a long pause and finally the eye contact I had been searching for. The fact of the matter was, it WASN'T me. I knew I had been a great, astute boyfriend. My side of the street was clean, and I had carried my weight well in the relationship. Not to mention I had twenty little paper cuts on my hands because the night before I had made 347 origami roses for him until three a.m. (dumb things hipster twenty-five-year-olds apparently do) to prove my devotion. I was *not* taking the blame for this. I had also been the best *goy*-friend any Jewish guy could ask for. I eagerly attended *all* the obligatory Jewish holiday gatherings on Long Island his family threw, and with bells on! Present and participatory with genuine fervor, I fasted out of solidarity. I drank the Manisch-ewitz. I chatted with Aunt Helen time and again about her collection of dachshund figurines and I ate the gefilte fish (both of which he himself would usually refuse to partake in, might I add).

Finally, I started to absorb more of what he was saying. For better or for worse, he was beginning to find his words. Maybe a bit too many of them. He proceeded to tell me how he needed to focus more on his career and how I should focus on mine as well. He continued, explaining that I was only the second relationship he'd ever been in and that maybe he needed to sow more oats.

My grandma always told me to be suspicious of laundry lists of conflicting excuses. She said that when someone means well or is telling the truth and devoid of guilt, one reason does the job. Let me also be clear, he just wasn't a wild oats kind of guy. He's a "Let's get wacky and eat Chinese food in bed, drink Tsingtao, and watch *The Comeback* before falling asleep at eleven-twenty p.m." kind of guy.

Simmering with hostility, I stared down at my last meatball, imagining it to be his handsome little head, and jabbed the fucker with a fork. Then I put the entire ball into my mouth. Chewing forcefully, for a moment I thought that maybe as a last resort I should try to choke on it. That way, maybe I would really have a chance to be saved by "Grandpa." Or better, maybe I'd just die and be put out of my misery— death by meatball! (Imagine the ball puns the *New York Post* would revel in.) But no, keeping my tears at bay, I just continued chewing for an unprecedented thirty-seven seconds because even when life drops the ball, you simply must eat the ball—all of it. Then cry when you get home.

I really should have "focused on myself" and my own life, but when has anyone ever actually taken the advice of their heartbreaker? I spent the next few days (um . . . weeks) talking about the breakup and seeking insight from anyone who would listen. It was like I was trying to go on some sort of masochistic breakup treasure hunt for the reason why it happened. I was even deranged enough to think that at the end of my quest, I would have all the answers (at least the ones I wanted to hear), and he would magically pop up out of the treasure box with confetti and streamers like a pinup lady in a cake. "I was wrong. I missed you," he would admit. "There's no one I would rather have by my side during my quarter-life crisis than you, Andrew!"

As it turns out, people were very much chomping at the bit to hear a Valentine's Day breakup story. Especially one that involved meatballs. *I'm sorry about your boyfriend and the meatball,* a friend wrote to me a few days after. *That sounds rough. He's just so nice. Who would have thought? I can't believe it!* I became great at telling it with equal parts bravado, angst, and humor. My new defense mechanism was to really hone my material, to find my inner stand-up and make people laugh along with me. If I did that, I could make it through the whole tale without crying.

I must have recounted the night about 460 times, even writing a short story about it, where I inexplicably made the characters lesbians (perhaps also file that under more dumb things twenty-five-year-old tangential hipsters do). But I never found the treasure. If a "nice" guy breaks your heart, apparently, you don't ever hear the words you need. When a nice guy breaks your heart, you finish last.

A few weeks after we split, I stumbled upon clues from mutual friends that he was dating a midlevel marketing guy in publishing. *Some wild oats,* I thought to myself.

Considering this ever-so-slightly predates the dawn of social media, there was no easy way to stalk your ex-boyfriends, not to mention their new boyfriends. So unless you physically stalked them while hiding in a plant, you would have to wait until that one evening when you felt almost okay for a moment. This, then, allowed a nosy shit-stirrer, who was almost always masked as a concerned friend, to call you to tell you they're shocked to have met the new boyfriend of the man who broke you into pieces.

The night I received this call, I learned my replacement was prematurely bald, had buck teeth, and smiled frantically throughout the night, even though he apparently barely spoke. I was told that from an optics standpoint they already seemed like an old married couple. It was apparent the marketing guy had been in the picture for a while, and it was confirmed that it actually wasn't, in fact, me, but him all along. Moreover, if he had given me the dignity of replacing me with a twinky twenty-year-old model, I might have been able to wrap my head around *those* oats.

The funny thing about rock bottom is that it's never the true bottom. There are always little trapdoors with subbasements and cellars you didn't know existed. I had just fallen into one. Despite the fact that I'm a bad liar and a Goody Two-shoes, I told work I had jury duty. I spent the next ten days barely leaving the house and becoming emotionally invested in marathons of reality TV, a vice I had surprisingly never succumbed to before.

On one of those nights, an unexpected snowstorm had swept through the city, and I let the day get past me. Way too late, I realized I had nothing to eat for dinner. I did, however, have a fridge that was 90 percent full of condiments and a marginally nice bottle of prosecco. I scoured the cupboards like an archaeological dig. I discovered a jar of cloves I didn't know why I had, a tin of sardines, a carton of coconut milk, and then an actual treasure: a forgotten can of "uh-oh" SpaghettiOs with meatballs. I had forgotten that I keep one stashed to provide added comfort or as a kind of immediate triage in case of sickness and/or a debilitating hangover.

Despite growing up in the 1980s, when processed food was unavoidable, my mom made a conscious effort to feed me and my brothers the opposite of processed food. Everything was usually homemade and very fresh. However, she swayed the rules on snow days, or when I was home sick from school, and, of course, on fantasy dinner night. Fantasy dinner night was a sporadic occurrence where, as a family, we would go on an impromptu trek to the grocery store just before dinnertime. Each of us got to choose whatever we wanted to eat. It could be lobster, TV dinners, ice cream, Cocoa Krispies, or canned sloppy joe mix filled with all the additives and preservatives your little heart desired. Like jury duty (real or faux), you never really knew when fantasy dinner night was going to happen.

On what would be my last night of being self-sequestered, so to speak, in my tiny East Village kitchenette, I stood heating the unearthed can of high-fructose-infused rings and tiny meatballs in a saucepan.

I carefully poured the SpaghettiOs into a blue Vancouver 1986 World Expo mug (the vessel one should *always* serve SpaghettiOs in), popped the prosecco, and made a wish (one should *always* make a wish when popping a cork), ambitiously drinking the prosecco directly from the bottle, and taking a big relentless sip. Wiping the sparkling stream that was now running down my chin, I proceeded to carefully blow on the cluster of steamy, unnaturally orange-hued piquant circles polka-dotted by a mini meatball that I had ladled up.

Isn't it curious that when we are either extremely happy or in supreme pain that we turn to the same food for assurance *and*, more important, reassurance? It was time to reframe and regain custody of these reliable, albeit heavily artificially preserved balls on my own now *very* bite-size terms (and, in a way, my innocence in the process). I took a bite. It was going to be okay. I was going to be okay. I'm okay.

"Uh-oh" SpaghettiOs with Meatballs

SERVES 1

Peak SpaghettiOs with meatballs enjoyment usually requires self-confinement.

This guilty pleasure 1965 time capsule on a plate is generally best paired with melancholia, tender hangovers and/or breakups, inclement weather, waiting for a direct deposit, Armageddon (in the literal sense as well as the 1998 sci-fi film), Saturday nights in (a rebellious act for any New Yorker), and après anxiety attacks (light to medium in scale). They are not only an excellent option for a makeshift fantasy dinner night but also pretty much the only acceptable meal one can buy at a twenty-four-hour CVS, and for $1.79 at that.

1. Open using the pull tab on top of the can. While this may resemble a can of tuna or cat food, it's more convenient than waiting five minutes for a can opener to "latch" like in the olden days. CAREFUL not to slice yourself with the lid, which has now precariously become a round razor blade.

2. While you may be pleasantly surprised by the acceptable calorie count of the entire can, you mustn't *ever* pay attention to the total milligrams of sodium or carbohydrates on the label.

3. Likewise, it's imperative that you *never* look at the list of incomprehensible, inorganic ingredients (many of which sound as if they are from a periodic table from hell) or even begin to decipher the difference between *chicken* and *mechanically separated chicken* (both of which are included).

4. Plop the contents into a smallish saucepan. After taking a moment to question why *saucepan* is one word, use a spoon to scrape the remaining stubborn rings and balls that seem to be holding out for a hero from the shadowy depths of the can.

5. Take a fun look at the orange stains on the sides of the steel cylinder. If you're lucky, your insides will soon be that color.

6. Heat on the stove on medium-high (low heat if more self-reflection is needed or if you like to pretend that you are actually cooking).

7. Regardless of the time of day, turn off any overhead lighting and light a candle for ambience—preferably a taper. They quickly give any shitty meal or shitty apartment an immense dose of ye olde world European charm and coziness.

8. Select piano-driven, midcentury jazz music by Dave Brubeck, Sonny Clark, Oscar Peterson, or Ahmad Jamal, to be played preferably on vinyl, though placing an iPhone in an empty water glass works just fine.

9. Using a wooden spoon, stir occasionally.

10. Have one existential thought per every three rotations or completely zone out into a meditative state the entire time.

11. There's nothing wrong with putting lipstick on a pig—everyone loves a makeover. Time to bring this drugstore diamond of a meal to its full potential. Add two squirts of sriracha (do a test squeeze in the kitchen sink first, as the first squeeze is usually quite overzealous), freshly slapped basil when available, and a dash of everything bagel seasoning, depending on how sassy you're feeling.

12. Once the SpaghettiOs and balls begin to emit gurgles and steam, pour them into a vintage novelty, or super chunky, ceramic mug (preferably one that would resemble something Joni Mitchell or Diane Keaton would have used in 1978). An oversize cup-and-saucer combo from the 1990s is perfectly acceptable as well.

13. Take out an old bottle of cheap prosecco someone brought over for a cocktail party a few weeks ago or that expensive bottle of champagne your boss or client sent that you've been saving for a year (luxury really does go with everything, after all). Make a wish and pop the cork. Pour into a coupe glass, mug, teacup, or even a juice tumbler, but *never* a wineglass.

14. Conjuring the voice of a middle-aged waiter, ask, "Pepper?" "Yes, thank you, that would be lovely." Proceed to grind the pepper over the SpaghettiOs with a flourish.

15. While the SpaghettiOs and meatballs may appear ready to eat, *proceed with caution*. Go to the next point for the reason why.

16. *You may have a cold heart*, yet these li'l rings are somehow able to retain an implausibly significant amount of piping lava-like heat much greater than their weight would infer. Therefore, it's vital that *before each bite*, you blow on every tangy and gummy (yes, gummy, it's part of their 1960s Sally Draper charm), high-fructose-corn-syrup–induced spoonful *twice* (in two-second increments) throughout the meal so you don't get burned—you've got enough "uh-ohs" to deal with. The blowing is an act of self-care for the heart and all its cockles.

SOLYANKA VALENTINA

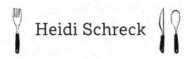

Heidi Schreck

IN 1994, I MOVED TO A TINY TOWN IN SIBERIA TO TEACH EN-
glish for a few months and ended up living in Russia for almost
three years because I fell in love with a man and his mother. Actually, I loved the mother, Valentina Konstantinovna, first and possibly
best. She was a retired engineer with a radiant, gap-toothed smile who
whooshed into my classroom one morning like a psychedelic Mary
Poppins in an electric-blue kaftan with a matching skullcap, and an-
nounced she was designing costumes for my production of *Macbeth*.
Until she materialized, seemingly out of air, I did not think my students
would be wearing costumes or that what we were doing qualified as a
"production." We were playing around with a silly ESL adaptation of
Macbeth in class because I was sick of hearing my students recite Robert
Burns's "A Red, Red Rose" from their Soviet-era textbooks. I'm not
sure who told Valentina about our project, but she had *opinions* and

demanded I come to her flat for dinner so she could tell me every one of them.

We talked for hours that first night about witchcraft, evil, and whether Lady Macbeth was clinically depressed over steaming bowls of something called solyanka, a thick, salty-sour soup, crammed with too many kinds of meat and also . . . pickles. Valentina said it was a soup you made when your fridge was overflowing with a bunch of chaotic, aging leftovers you needed to transform before they turned rancid, and that, for this reason, it was also called "soup of a woman's soul." I'm pretty sure she made that up because I never heard anyone else call it this, but her feminine chaos theory made sense to me. I was twenty-two and a hormonal, grieving mess. We drank vodka with our soup, and after a few shots I sobbed to her that my boyfriend back home had just dumped me for another girl and then made me look at a picture of her so I could assure him she was pretty. (I did.) Also, I was on a new birth control pill that made me want to smash windows with my fists. Valentina poured me another shot and confessed that she was in a similar transitional storm, whirling in the eye of a menopausal hurricane. The last of her kids had just left for college and her husband was living in another town, possibly with another woman. And so Valentina and I spent the next three years baring our own chaotic souls to each other, over hundreds of the most pleasurable meals I have ever eaten.

We each spoke the other's language poorly, so we shouted and mimed at each other while she showed me how to make borscht and cucumber salad and crisp potato vareniky fried in butter in her wee kitchen. She was fanatic about teaching me to cook so that when I got back home I would be self-sufficient. In her opinion, I needed to "взять себя в руки," which basically meant "take myself in my own arms." When she said this, I pictured wrapping my arms around myself and whispering *shhhhhh*, like I was a baby and also the baby's mother. Once, I tried to teach her how to make my mom's lasagna, but we couldn't find the right kind of cheese or noodles in Siberia, so it emerged from the oven a lumpen pile of crap, and when Valentina helped me pull it from the oven, I accidentally slammed the door shut on her arm. She screamed obscenities I don't know how to translate, then ran cold water over the burn and smiled at me, and said, "Stop feeling like shit! Now I have something to remember you by."

After our dinners, we watched VHS tapes of classic Soviet musicals and planned our *Macbeth*. A young man named Otari sometimes came over to play Chopin on the creaky piano while we sliced red fabric into ribbons for King Duncan to pull from his shirt after Macbeth stabbed him. The music gave Valentina an idea: "You're going to be the accompanist for our production, Otari! You're going create a mood of horror!"

Otari shrugged. "Okay."

Our *Macbeth* debuted in the spring of 1995 to a polite audience of parents in the high school gym. Otari improvised a spooky live score. Dima, our Macbeth, dragged dead King Duncan in by the feet to show his wife he'd "done the deed," and Natstya, playing all of the witches, hopped around shrieking in a three-faced mask. I'm not sure it's possible to say any of the actors were "good" by aesthetically normative standards, but I remember that fifteen-year-old Olga brought all of her adolescent fury and angst and authentic bitchiness to the role of Lady Macbeth and that when she entered, the audience members went still for a few moments, their attention finally caught by some unexpected flicker of truth. And . . . what else? That time is fading for me. I've forgotten so many names and faces and voices, they glimmer for me now in what the poet Anna Akhmatova called "the second age of memory" where ". . . the sky glows pink, / Names of cities change / And there are no remaining witnesses to the events, / And no one to weep with . . ."

I remember . . . what? That Yeltsin was president. That Leningrad had changed its name back to St. Petersburg, but people still called it Leningrad. And that one day, Valentina's twenty-nine-year-old son, Sergei, arrived from Novosibirsk, and I fell in love with him too. Valentina was furious with both of us but only punished her son for our transgression. She refused to speak to him for weeks except to shout, "You're always stealing my friends!" and yet all the while she and I continued to make blini and cold cucumber soups and pelmeni together like nothing had happened. And then one morning, she decided the three of us were going to get on a train to St. Petersburg to start a new life alongside her brilliant daughters, who were in college there.

The story of our life in St. Petersburg is long, and I cannot recount it here, in part because so many of the details are lost to me. I can say the years I spent living with Valentina and her three children were wonderful, abundant with love, with food and music and art, and with more than a few tearful arguments. "I'm going to haunt you!" she liked to say in the middle of a fight, and she was right. Though she died almost a decade ago, I still hear her voice telling me to read Akhmatova when I am caught in a riptide of sadness and to never sit on the cold ground unless I want my ovaries to freeze. When I catch a whiff of dill or dump a bunch of leftover crap into a pot to make a comforting solyanka, I think of her blue eyes sparkling and her forearms bedecked with cooking scars, including the one I gave her. Valentina still lives in my first age of memory, the one of which Akhmatova said, "The tears stream still, the peals of laughter linger, / The spot of ink still stains the desk, and, sealed / Upon the heart, the farewell kiss remains, / Indelible. . . ."

Solyanka Valentina

6 or 7 slices of bacon, chopped, or ⅓ cup of cubed salo
1 pound thinly sliced beef chuck or sirloin
½ cup cubed kielbasa or hard salami
1 cup cubed ham
2 medium onions, chopped
2 medium carrots, chopped
1 stalk celery, thinly sliced
½ cup shredded green cabbage
1 cup pitted black or green Gordal olives
6 tablespoons tomato paste
1 teaspoon paprika
4 whole black peppercorns
3 whole allspice berries
1 (28-ounce) can whole peeled tomatoes in juice, crushed
1 teaspoon khmeli suneli (or 1 bay leaf)
5 cups beef stock
2 or 3 large dill pickles, chopped
1½ tablespoons capers
Kosher salt and freshly ground black pepper
½ lemon, sliced
Chopped parsley, sliced scallions, fresh dill, and sour cream

Fry the bacon (or salo) in a large soup pot over medium heat. When the bacon starts to crisp, remove it with a slotted spoon and set it aside. Add the beef, kielbasa (or salami), and ham to the pot and cook over medium heat for 6 to 8 minutes, or until the meat browns.

Take the meat out of the pot and set aside on a plate. Remove all but a couple of tablespoons of the leftover fat from the pot. Sauté the onions in the pot for around 3 to 4 minutes, or until they start to soften. Add the carrots, celery, cabbage, and olives (saving some for garnish), and cook everything for another 3 minutes.

Move the veggies to the side, add the tomato paste, and cook for another 3 minutes. Add the paprika, peppercorns, and allspice, and stir everything together. Return the beef, kielbasa (or salami), and ham to the pot, along with the tomatoes and khmeli suneli (or bay leaf).

Return the bacon to the pot, add the beef stock, and bring to a boil. Reduce the heat to medium-low or low and add the pickles and capers. Simmer for 3½ to 4 hours, or until the beef is tender. Season with salt and pepper to taste. Serve your solyanka with slices of lemon, parsley, scallions, fresh dill, and a spoonful of sour cream, and plop a couple of olives on top.

JELL-O CAKE

 Andrew Rannells

WHEN I WAS GROWING UP, IT WAS PART OF OUR FAMily tradition that for your birthday celebration, you got to pick dinner and the cake. I usually picked Chinese food from a restaurant in Omaha called King Fong's. Sadly, they have closed, but I still think about their egg rolls and fried rice. And without fail, every year for my birthday, I asked for the same cake.

We were not a family for store-bought desserts. We would order takeout, but when it came to dessert, especially birthday cakes, those were always homemade. The cake choosing was always easy for me. I would always ask my mother to make a Jell-O cake.

You might be wondering, "Is this a cake made of Jell-O?" If you are wondering this, you are not from the Midwest. I don't know where the recipe came from. I'm assuming the back of a box of Jell-O in the seventies, or maybe from a *McCall's* magazine or an article in *Parade*.

The concept is simple: You take a box cake mix and make it as instructed. Duncan Hines, Betty Crocker, they all work. Vanilla or white cake is best, but I suppose you could try others. My mom always made two layers. Usually round. I didn't know that this was sort of fancy. When I got older and realized that some families just made sheet cakes in a 9 × 13-inch pan, I understood that my mother must really love me because she always made two 8-inch circular cakes. The stack is lovely—it takes a little more effort, but you get more frosting, kids!

Once the cakes are done, here's where it gets wacky. Leave them in the pans. Make a box of Jell-O as directed on the box, just to the liquid stage. I always chose lime for my birthday because my favorite color is green, but you can use any flavor. I've had success with multiple varieties.

For the next step, the cakes don't have to be cool, but also don't burn yourself. Using a toothpick or barbecue skewer, gently poke holes through the top of the cake. Not too many, but not too few. Try to go for a unified pattern if possible. Follow the edge of the pan and work inward.

Then gently pour the liquid Jell-O onto the cake. Don't go too quickly, you don't want to overwhelm the poor thing, you just want the Jell-O to seep into the cake through the holes you have lovingly made. Keep an eye on your portions if you are using two cakes (as I hope you are) because one box of Jell-O should get you through two 8-inch round cakes.

Once the Jell-O is administered into the cakes, place the cakes in the refrigerator to cool and set. This will take several hours. Let's say three.

Once cooled and set, you can *gently* remove the cakes from their pans. I'll be honest: I've cracked a lot of cakes in the process. It's a real shame, but if it happens to you, don't panic! You are going to frost these babies and no one will see the cracks.

Frosting . . . here's where it gets wild. "What will I frost these Jell-O beauties with?" you might be thinking. Well, I'll tell you . . . Cool Whip. That's right. This whole damn recipe can be achieved with convenience items. Most everything you need is from a box or a tub. You're welcome! Slather that Cool Whip onto the cakes and layer them as desired. Cool Whip is a tricky lady, so you are going to have to take your time. Sometimes little pieces of cake flip up into the Cool Whip, which is sad. But to that I say, just add more Cool Whip! Cover those mistakes up!

With your cake complete, shove it back in the fridge to set. Jell-O cake is best served cold.

It's a simple recipe with no fancy ingredients. No technical skill is required to pull it off. But every time my mom made it for me, I felt like the luckiest guy in the world. Yes, it's a box cake, but there are extra steps one has to take to make it into a Jell-O cake.

I think it's still my favorite dessert.

JELL-O CAKE

GO FIGURE

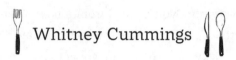

Whitney Cummings

"FIGS ARE GREAT FOR FERTILITY," MY GRANDMOTHER said.

Sure, fine, but they are also great for . . . food? I was seven when I had my first fig. Well, technically, it was a Fig Newton. I was obsessed with Fig Newtons. The commercials were so intense: "A cookie is just a cookie, but a Fig Newton is *fruit and cake*." Fruit *and* cake?! For a dollar?! This was a very big deal. As a kiddo I wasn't into sweets; the only ones I'd entertain were candy corn and Cow Tales. I know. I think that last sentence is on the list of "how to spot a psychopath," but for me, for a treat to be a treat, it had to have a consistency that I could really savor. It had to be velvety and viscous. I liked to gnaw, to chew, and I sometimes hoped the treat would get stuck in my back teeth so I could taste it all day long. Honestly, I'm starting to think I really might be a psychopath. But this is about figs.

Fig Newtons: Fruit. And. Cake. Excuse me? It just sounded so fancy. Like, I feel like if Marie Antoinette were reincarnated into RuPaul today, that's what she would have eaten. A Fig Newton. I mean, the words alone—Newton was a revered mathematician, and *fig* just felt very fashionable to me, like very cool and Italian . . . kind of a close relative to *twiggy* . . . *twig* . . . *fig*. This may also be because when I was young, if things rhymed I just assumed they were related somehow. Although my obsession with rhymes, alliteration, and double entendres came to a screeching halt when I realized my last name was Cummings. I always knew it was Cummings. But it wasn't till I was in high school that I found out that my last name was an epic bummer.

"But, Whitney? Aren't your parents divorced? Why don't you just take your mother's maiden name?"

That's a great question with a not-so-great answer. My mom's maiden name is Cumming. With no *s*. My dad's was Cummings. I know. It's a lot to process. But I totally get how when they met it must have been a love-at-first-trauma bond. Two lost souls finally finding someone who shared the embarrassment of having a last name that was an iteration of cum.

I digress, but I'm also weirdly somehow on theme because this piece is about figs, the fruit that symbolizes fertility, or fruit-ility, if you will, given I've already admitted my penchant for puns. The first time I had a Fig Newton, I almost collapsed. To this day when I eat a Fig Newton, I brace myself so I don't throw out my neck saying, "Oh my God why is this so good? I don't want this to be over!"

While I battled a Fig Newton addiction in high school, that battle was soon eclipsed by an eating disorder. Once my brain persuaded itself that I needed to be alarmingly thin to get the approval of men I didn't even like or respect, my dear Fig Newtons got the boot. But the good news was that Fig Newtons were fruit *and* cake. So, as someone who was suddenly terrified of carbohydrates, I could at least have the fruit part. No cake.

Enter the dried fig. Dried figs came in the most elegant tight rolls or, because they became slightly trendy for a minute, given their fibrous properties, sometimes a glossy bag. I started to see bags of dried figs in the raisin section, which always made me think of figs as pregnant raisins. I know that's odd, but then again, "Figs are great for fertility." But also, figs are weird! Dried figs look like old aliens. Let's be honest, they also look like little ball sacs. When hanging on trees, they just look like young ball sacs. It's not great. (But oh my God, they are so great.) Regardless, they always look very exhausted. Figs may not be the oldest fruit on Earth, but they certainly look the most tired.

Regardless, it seems like figs have been relegated to the ranks of polarizing treats: licorice, olives, key lime, dried cherries on salad, and coffee ice cream. They're not for everyone. But neither am I. I guess maybe I relate to figs a little bit: we're not quite sweet, not quite salty, and we're both very tired.

All through college, I was obsessed with dried figs. It was such a perfect journey for me: take something with an ugly outside, put it in your mouth, and reveal the wonders of the inside. The metaphors literally never end.

I've always had a thing for crusted-around goopy things. Magic Middles, the gum with the goo inside, Cadbury Creme Eggs, Magic Shell. Maybe it's symbolic of me as a person, as a comedian, where I present a tough exoskeleton on the outside, but on the inside I'm secretly just a very sensitive marshmallow. Even though, oddly enough, I am not a marshmallow person. I do not get Peeps. I will die on this hill.

My journey with figs is not over yet, folks. I now have a fig tree in my yard. I am thirty-nine years old. I am at a point where I should decide if I want to have biological children or not. Because the fertility fig thing was imprinted on me when I was a kid by my grandmother, I always associated figs with having kids one day. Figs even kind of look like ovaries (and ball sacs).

Looking back, I don't think it's an accident that my eating disorder reared its head after I terminated a pregnancy at fifteen. And I don't think it's a coincidence that I gravitated toward figs, the fruit of fertility, as a comfort food. I mostly disassociated that time in my life—albeit I was able to recollect enough to write a chapter about it in my book— but I wasn't conscious enough to be making decisions that were congruous with any meaningful intention.

Like most women, the fertility issue is always dancing in the back of my mind. How much time do I have? Do I need to hurry? Have I missed my window? What if I never have biological kids? What if this is payback for my terminated pregnancy? You know, the hits! I've been to therapists, fertility doctors, and psychics, and, frankly, the most wisdom I have gleaned on this issue is from my beloved fig.

Every morning I make coffee, then walk out to the fig tree in my yard. I don't eat dried figs anymore unless it's a jam (also known as *my* jam) because I have real fresh figs. Sometimes they're ripe, sometimes they're not. I'll scope the tree out and see if there are any darker ones, feel them, see if any are getting soft; if they are hard, I'll decide if I want to go for it and start my day with a drier, tart situation or wait a couple of days and have a mushy sweet festival. I truly don't have a preference. Either way, they're good. If they're green, they're good; if they're purple, they're good; if they're hard, soft, whatever.

When I go into the doctor's office for fertility checks now and see my innards on a screen, I imagine my eggs as figs. Some are good, some not so good. But they're all good.

When I see my tree in the morning, I'm happy. If there are eight figs, I'm happy and will put them in a bowl to share; if there are two, I'm happy. I can't have high expectations because where I live, I'm not the only one who is obsessed with figs. Squirrels get them, rats, deer, coyotes; I often find them on the ground with bites taken out of them and think, "Thanks for sharing this fig with me, you fancy rat."

Whether I have kids or not, whether I can naturally conceive or not, whether I have to do IVF or adopt or get a surrogate, I'm good. Like my fig tree, my body will yield what it yields, and I'll be grateful for whatever I get.

Figs have become my daily reminder to live life on life's terms and to be happy with or without my biological or professional harvest. Whether I have huge career achievements or just a lazy day of self-restoration with my horse, I'm good. My tree reminds me that whatever comes my way or doesn't, I'll fig-ure it out.

COME ON! I HAD TO.

POPSICLE LOVE

 Michaela Jaé Rodriguez

I REMEMBER THE FIRST TIME I HAD A POPSICLE. IT WAS SWEET, it was juicy, and it was satisfying. Though store-bought, it still had a magic to it . . . but what if? What if I was able to create my own?

I was always the kid who had a sweet tooth, especially for natural sweets, like fruits. So, when I was fourteen and finally able to create my own first organic popsicle, boy, was I excited.

My mom had just bought me a popsicle maker. Shiny rubbery plastic. A bright cotton-candy blue! It was to die for!

I could've done it the old-fashioned way, through an ice tray, but I wanted a bigger portion, not to mention I knew it would look good in that popsicle maker!

I started with my fridge: there were two fresh batches of strawberries and one small tray of raspberries in there. I figured the ripe sweetness of strawberries and the tart sourness of raspberries would go well together. I grabbed seven strawberries and five raspberries, crushed them, and let them chill in the refrigerator. With a beaming smile on my face, I then rushed to the cabinet and grabbed vanilla extract and some agave syrup. I added one teaspoon of agave syrup and three drops of vanilla extract into a bowl filled with enough water for my six-slot popsicle tray.

I then added my chilled sweet-and-sour strawberries and raspberries, pouring them slowly into the mix that I created. I whipped together the ingredients as if they were potions in my cauldron. The fruity and syrupy smells blissfully coursed through my nose as I stirred. The magic of this creation was coming to fruition.

Last, I grabbed my shiny blue plastic popsicle tray, and I slowly poured the juicy, thick, sappy concoction into each of the six slots. It was quite easy to put the wooden sticks in—they stood up perfectly. Then, with stars in my eyes, I opened the freezer and placed them inside. I knew they wouldn't be frozen within just a couple of hours, so I waited a full day for them to completely freeze.

And then, *voilà!* My first organic strawberry and raspberry popsicles were complete! The taste was so sweet and not overbearingly sour. The hints of vanilla and agave appeased my taste buds just the way they needed to. My popsicles were a success! I knew from then on that this was a recipe I would re-create for years to come. What a way to enjoy the summer!

MICHAELA JAÉ RODRIGUEZ

MISSION: JIRO

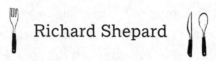

Richard Shepard

I LOVE MOVIES, AND I LOVE FOOD.

And I particularly love movies about food.

Big Night is a mouthwatering foray into classic Italian cooking via 1950s New Jersey. *Tampopo* is a delicious comedy that fetishizes ramen noodles into a religion. Even Peter Greenaway's darkly gluttonous cannibalistic orgy—*The Cook, the Thief, His Wife & Her Lover*—gets the taste buds humming.

That said, my favorite food-centric film is David Gelb's documentary *Jiro Dreams of Sushi*, about one of Japan's premier sushi chefs, Jiro Ono, who has worked for decades in an anonymous restaurant located in a Tokyo subway station. It's a precise and delicious love letter to one man's lifelong journey in pursuit of culinary perfection. One indelible and deeply edible bite at a time.

After seeing that film, my girlfriend, Jenni—now my wife—and

I became obsessed, like almost everyone who saw the documentary, with this eighty-five-year-old sushi master. We both shared the dream of someday going to Tokyo and eating the food that Jiro himself created. The fact that it was nearly impossible to get a reservation at that restaurant was beside the point—Jenni, the woman whom I loved more than anyone in the world, wanted to eat at Jiro's restaurant, Sukiyabashi Jiro, and it became my goal, my *mission*, to secretly make that happen.

But how? Reservations were a near impossibility. They were booked months, even years, in advance. And I didn't speak any Japanese. And Jiro only spoke Japanese. I couldn't just call up. I needed a plan.

First, I decided to let my innate fear of spending money disappear like the morning fog over Mount Fuji. This was an important decision, mostly because this whole endeavor was going to be the most expensive four days of my life.

With that in mind, I picked a weekend six months in the future and quietly let Jenni's assistant know that she shouldn't schedule anything for Jenni in the days surrounding it.

And then—because money was no object—I booked a room at the Four Seasons in Tokyo. I knew that the hotel catered to a wealthy and influential clientele, and if anyone could help me get a reservation at Sukiyabashi Jiro, it would be them. Plus I could cancel if they struck out, thus keeping my money, which, as I said, was of no object but was obviously of object.

As I asked the hotel's concierge for help making the reservation at Jiro's restaurant, I could hear his polite but sad "I feel sorry for you" sigh over the phone. I knew we weren't the first visitors to request his help on this particular matter. The film was incredibly popular and reservation requests were coming in fast and furious (eventually President

Obama would venture into the subway station and eat there). Trying to be malleable, I told the concierge that we would be fine with lunch. With any time of day or night. I would show up at nine a.m. or at midnight. Whatever magic he could swing.

Of course, everything at Sukiyabashi Jiro was fully booked, but the Four Seasons concierge told me he would continue to try in case a cancellation happened. Each week I would email him, and each week he would email me back telling me that there still weren't any openings.

Weeks went by. Months.

And then, like tasting some heavenly piece of fatty toro, a miracle occurred. Just eight weeks before we were supposed to travel, I received an email from the concierge—

—A noon reservation for two at the sushi bar had opened up.

Sukiyabashi Jiro was ours.

I booked the flight and surprised Jenni with the news. As Bowie said, "We can be heroes just for one day."

As the travel date approached, we did our research. Nothing was left to chance. Jiro expected you to be on time. If you were even a minute late, he considered it rude. You weren't to wear cologne or perfume in the restaurant as any smell would compete with your ability to taste the sushi as he intended. You weren't allowed to take any photos. Jiro's restaurant was a serious, if simple, sushi experience. It wasn't a tourist destination, despite the fact that we were tourists destined to eat there.

Upon arrival in Tokyo (and dealing with a neon-lit jet lag that threw our minds into a blender) we decided to do a dry-run journey to the restaurant. It was only a few blocks from the hotel, but because the signage on the streets was impossible for us to read, we wanted to know exactly how to get to there, and how long it would take. Amazingly, it took just about six minutes to reach the subway entrance that housed the restaurant. Jenni and I smiled at each other—everything was falling perfectly into place.

Knowing Jiro's insistence on punctuality, on the day of the reservation, Jenni and I decided to leave ten minutes early, just to make sure nothing could go wrong. Maybe it was the time-zone turnaround that had made our heads cloudy, or the lights, sounds, and general beautiful strangeness of Tokyo, but as we were leaving the hotel on the big day, we were surprised to be told that there wasn't just one entrance to the subway station, there were eight, spread over several blocks, and we had gone to the wrong one in our dry run. The one we wanted—the one where Jiro made his sushi—was blocks farther up the street.

This was a disaster.

Suddenly our ten-minute window for a six-minute walk seemed extraordinarily tight.

Terrified that we would be late, we raced out of the hotel, speed walking like Olympic hopefuls. Actually, we weren't speed walking—after a few moments, we were running—sweat dripping down our faces as we ran. After all of this planning—we *needed* to be on time.

I held on to the map the concierge gave me with an iron grip. Left, right. Right. Left. Into the station—not that entrance—the other entrance—the one in the middle of the street. Down some stairs. To the right. To the left. It was now 11:59 a.m.

And then.

There was Sukiyabashi Jiro.

Just where it should be.

Sitting anonymously in the train station. A place you might not have even noticed. The best sushi restaurant in the world.

And there standing in the window—Jiro himself. Making rice. Stone-faced. Focused. Dreaming of sushi.

Jenni and I raced to the restaurant's door just as our iPhones hit twelve p.m. on the nose. A young man was there. "Mr. Shepard?" he asked, already knowing the answer. I don't know why it shocked us that they were expecting us, that they knew who we were, but it did. The young man led us into a completely empty restaurant. We were the only people there. Just us and Jiro, along with one of his sons (whom we recognized from the documentary), an older female hostess, and this young man in a starched white apron.

Jiro nodded, or at least I thought he did, and we were walked to the simple sushi bar to the left. There were about twelve chairs around the L-shaped sushi bar and that was it. There were also two empty booths against the wall.

We sat, nervously ordered two beers, and tried to collect our wits and breaths.

We had previously been told that you needed to eat Jiro's sushi within thirty seconds of it being placed in front of you because any longer and you would miss the exactitude of the meeting of Jiro's warm rice to the cold of his perfectly cut fish.

As we were the only people in the restaurant, and Jiro had no one else to cook for, our first piece of sushi arrived about two minutes after we were seated. Still sweating and barely able to have a sip of our cold beer, Jenni and I ate the sushi—no extra soy sauce, and with our hands, as was the custom—within moments of its arrival on the table, as instructed.

I think it was delicious, though honestly, I was still trying to stop my heart from racing.

The restaurant was absolutely silent. No music. No anything. The young man in the starched apron quietly brought out large pieces of fish from the refrigerator in the back. Jiro's son silently cut the fish. Jiro himself, like a Jedi master, wordlessly molded the rice, applied any soy sauce or wasabi, and then placed the perfectly cut fish on the rice and put the sushi on our plate.

Within a minute of our first pieces of sushi being eaten, another beautiful piece of fish was in front of us. Within thirty seconds it was in our mouths. A minute later, there was another piece. Thirty seconds later it was in our mouths again. This went on for about five minutes.

With every piece of fish, Jiro stared at us out of the corner of his eye. Like the best of poker players, you couldn't tell what he was thinking. But he was studying us, we knew that. He was judging.

I put up a good front, appearing to love the sushi, but the sad truth was that we were both so nervous, so wound up from the lead-up, that we could barely enjoy what we were eating. Intellectually, we knew that the fish was on another level, that the care and perfection of its presentation was a thing of singular beauty, but we couldn't center ourselves enough to let it all in.

It didn't help that the requisite quiet and stillness of the restaurant, as well as its chef's stony face, made the scene almost . . . funereal.

After about eight pieces of sushi, I wanted to have some ginger to cleanse my palate, and I needed my chopsticks to eat it.

The chopsticks were held together by a thin band of paper. With what seemed like all eyes on me, I tried to separate the chopsticks by pulling them apart from the band, but I couldn't. The paper wouldn't tear. I tried again, Still nothing. I was suddenly weak. Like Superman with kryptonite, I couldn't do the simplest things.

I felt a wave of embarrassment. Of culinary failure. Of disrespect to Jiro. Our host.

It was humiliating.

Just then, Jiro put down the rice in his hand and walked over toward me. I was sure he was going to take the incredibly sharp blade he used for cutting fish and slit my throat with it for disrespecting him and the entire Japanese culture. Jiro leaned over the sushi bar and carefully took the chopsticks from my hand. Then, with the simplest of movements, he effortlessly slid the paper off the two pieces of wood, instantly separating the chopsticks.

Then he laughed. The sweetest laugh I have ever heard.

And soon the hostess and his son laughed. And the young man in the starched apron laughed.

It wasn't a mocking laugh coming from Jiro—it was—can I say it? A laugh of love?

And Jenni and I laughed too.

And then we all laughed together.

And, suddenly, everything was right with the world.

Suddenly, we could breathe the air. We could enjoy the experience.

We could taste Jiro's beautiful, impossibly perfect sushi.

Each bite after that became an explosion of flavor, texture, care, love, heaven, and hell. The clouds parted and the hands of God were making us this lunch.

Suddenly, the door opened . . .

Another couple walked in. Tourists like us. Only late.

It was twelve minutes after noon, and Jiro was having nothing to do with their tardiness. He quietly spoke to his son in Japanese and then walked away from this couple before they were even seated. He would not be involved in feeding them at all, and it fell to his son to deal with them. Jiro was still making sushi for us, but for his other guests who were late, he would not raise a finger.

And then another couple came in. They were also obviously late, and the woman was wearing perfume. The air filled with her scent, instead of the culinary scents that Jiro wanted to spark our senses. Jiro was again displeased. He once more spoke with his son, and again made clear that he wanted nothing to do with these new guests.

He would take their money and have his son make them sushi. But not the sushi Jiro dreamed about.

That sushi was special.

That sushi came only for us.

By 12:20 p.m. we had had twenty pieces of sushi—one a minute—and we were done with our meal.

Jiro gave the slightest of bows, a shy conductor of perfect, beautiful symphonies.

By this point, Japanese businessmen—regular customers, clearly, whose tardiness was not an issue—had filled the remaining empty seats of the bar. The hostess motioned Jenni and me away from the sushi bar and toward one of the two booths in the place. We weren't sure what awaited us there. We just sat obediently as two cups of steaming-hot tea were placed in front of us.

Moments later, the hostess came out with two perfect slices of melon. We smiled and mangled "Arigato," and then we cautiously

tasted this unbelievable fruit. It was like nothing I had ever had before. It hit my tongue like a cyclone, destroying all vestiges of previous melons in its path. It was a Molotov cocktail of flavor. Igniting and seducing our senses like a heated lover in one's dreams. What the hell was it? How could a piece of fruit be that . . . *delicious*?

We later found out it was a Crown muskmelon. A melon whose tree was picked bare so only this one melon got all the nutrients, all the flavor. Only this one remaining melon was loved and grown and picked at its absolute perfect ripeness.

After our last bites of melon were savored and our tea finished, the hostess quietly brought us the check.

It was the most expensive meal either of us had ever had. And it had taken all of thirty-five minutes.

After paying and thanking the hostess (Jiro himself was busy with his businessmen patrons), we were led out the front door by the young man in the starched white apron. Once outside the small restaurant, standing in the subway station, Jenni and I looked at each other. We felt a sense of accomplishment come over us, as if we had climbed Mount Everest without oxygen. We had somehow done it. Yes, it was wildly expensive. Yes, we had barely been able to enjoy the meal because we were so nervous. It didn't matter. It had all been worth it.

As the door was closing, I turned back to the young man. Would it be okay, I asked, if I took a selfie with Jenni outside? I knew that Jiro didn't allow photos inside his restaurant, but I thought the public area outside was fair game. Still, I wanted to ask. I wanted to make sure we didn't insult Jiro at this final juncture.

The young man smiled nervously and signaled to us to wait a moment. He then sped inside, obviously to check with Jiro himself if it was okay. Jenni and I shared a smile. What a crazy half hour we had just had.

Just then—Jiro himself came to the door.

He nodded at us, and then motioned for me to give my camera to the young man in the starched apron.

Jiro was not only allowing us to take a photograph—he wanted to be in it with us.

And as we smiled with this small, uniquely talented, and passionate man, we knew that it was his thank-you to us.

We had followed the rules he had set up perfectly. We had respected his art form.

And we had loved his food.

And for that, he gave us all the dreams he had in the world.

THE HYPE MACHINE

Alaina Moore

MANHATTAN'S SKYLINE TURNS OUT TO BE EXACTLY AS advertised. The cartoonishly tall buildings, the noise, the filth. To my uninitiated eyes, the city is as imposing as its reputation. Though I try to take it all in, my brain is porridge. Tonight is the biggest show of my band's first tour, and nervous anticipation has ruined several nights' sleep. As we inch through gridlocked streets on our way to sound check, one intersection blends meaninglessly into the next, and I can already feel myself forgetting.

Only a month earlier, Patrick and I were sitting on our living room floor labeling five hundred 7-inches. Their barely perceptible grooves bore the imprint of the first songs we had written. The preorder sold out before the records went into production. This stunned us. What began as a pastime—husband and wife making music together on weekends—cohered into realness seemingly overnight.

At work one morning, a friend rushed in, breathless from riding his bike.

"You're number one on Hype Machine!"

"What's Hype Machine?" I asked.

"You don't even know?" He gestured at the sky in frustration. "She doesn't even *know*."

After my shift, Patrick and I searched the blog aggregator. Our song "Marathon" had been written about so many times by so many publications, it would take hours to read it all. We were the most written-about band on the internet.

Something was happening, but it wasn't clear what until a Sony label executive showed up at Patrick's work and asked, "Are you Patrick Riley from the band Tennis?" That night, over a steak dinner at Elway's, he offered us a record deal.

It was too soon—we hadn't played a single show. We declined the offer, but we were determined not to waste the momentum. Patrick cold-called clubs and art collectives across the Midwest and Northeast until he had pieced together a small tour. As we loaded guitar amps into the back of our drummer's pickup truck, there was a shared sense of destiny—a feeling that our privately held dreams might find a home in the world.

Singing in church did not prepare me for the expectant gaze of a hundred hipsters. Onstage, I am surprised to discover that the spotlight has an antithetical, vanishing effect. In Omaha, my voice cracks. In Des Moines, my hands shake. In Chicago, I have dry mouth and facial spasms. The easy confidence I had in our practice space has abandoned me.

Patrick pulls me aside before our set in Boston. "Just have fun out there, Alaina. This is supposed to be fun."

I hoped the shows would get easier, but they don't. By the time we pull up to Cake Shop on New York's Lower East Side, I am a raw nerve.

The venue is a subterranean box, concrete with low ceilings. The stage in back is an even smaller box raised a few inches off the ground. I shuffle gear around aimlessly, doing things just to do them. Nothing about the rituals of sound check are instinctive. The endless cables, the jargon, the etiquette between band and house crew—all of it eludes me.

Patrick stomps a pedal, unmuting his guitar. "The promoter told me tonight is sold out. Sold out, Alaina!"

"Look at this." I hold up a free copy of *The Onion*. Under the header "Things to Do in NYC," our show is recommended alongside a solo set by The Killers' front man, Brandon Flowers. This is the first time we've seen our band name in print.

Patrick smiles. "Someone from Sub Pop is coming tonight. And *The New York Times*, and Jagjaguwar, *Pitchfork* . . ."

"Great." I say. "That's. Just. Great." I set up my keyboard like one assembling their own guillotine. "Our first New York show will be to a room full of critics."

I follow Patrick onstage without looking up. Anxiety billows off me in sheets. In the August heat my hair doubles in size. I try to make my face appear serene, or at least neutral, as I peek over my keyboard at the front row. The room is either loud or silent with anticipation. Through the blown-out light, I see one woman's face. We lock eyes and she smiles.

After our set, the room empties out. The promoter finds me and shakes my hand, beaming. "The last time we had a crowd like that, it was for Vampire Weekend."

It's late when Patrick leads me to a bar nearby. His arms are around me, and I walk without feeling the pavement. We could be ascending into space.

We sit at the bar top, our bodies canted lightly toward each other. On the drinks menu, I see *Manhattan*. I've never had one, but I order it without thinking. A slender coupe glass full of amber liquid resolves before me. It doesn't matter what it tastes like. I've already decided to love it.

"This is happening." Patrick says. "Do you want it to happen?"

I do. I'm ready.

Manhattan

2 parts rye whiskey or bourbon
1 part sweet vermouth*
Dash of bitters
Brandied cherry, for garnish

Combine ingredients with ice in a cocktail shaker and chill for one minute. Shake or stir vigorously. Strain into a coupe glass. Garnish with a brandied cherry.

---

*The vermouth is as important as the whiskey. Carpano Antica is the gold standard. Refrigerate vermouth after opening.

DONUT GO GENTLE

 Hamish Linklater

ND WHAT ABOUT SOMETHING SWEET?"

It's 2018. I'm standing at the counter of Fuel, on Main Street in Great Barrington, Massachusetts, on the way to visit Dennis, my godfather, who will be dead soon.

It's the day after Thanksgiving, my favorite holiday. The one I always head home for. The holiday of excess—too much food, booze, friends, and family—the holiday of self-punitive hyperindulgence. The holiday of bloat. That Thanksgiving we'd done it again, overdone it, and then done it some more.

And now I have three random hot beverages for my dying godfather, his wife, and myself in a drink caddy, and the fucking Fuel barista/sadist has taken the full measure of my greasy, sweat-steaming, oil-eyed regret and asked if I have just a *little room remaining* for something sweet.

This is the email exchange I had with Tina (Dennis's wife) the week prior:

> **TINA:** How would Friday at 11:30 be? The hospice nurse comes 10:30–11:30. If you could come then, I could slip away for half an hour at 11:45 and go to the gym (I'm desperate for breaks) and I'd be right back. Den's mind comes and goes. Sometimes he's his old witty, generous self; sometimes he can't follow the plot. But there's mountains of notes on his new project around *The Elizabethan World Picture* to read. He really wants to see you. A completion, if I can put it like that. Lol Tina.
>
> **ME:** Perfect. Anything I can arrive with? Coffee? Anything sweet? Rumi?
>
> **TINA:** Latte. Rumi good. Just in case. It might come up.

Step one in a Recipe for Disaster when going to visit a dying god-relation: Promise Rumi when you can't deliver.

On my way out to Dennis's that morning after Thanksgiving, I re-check the emails to confirm the time of the meeting and realize I've completely forgotten the promised Rumi, *The Essential Rumi*, that gold, black, and white spine as common to a bookshelf as floss to a bathroom. I search frantically, but there is no *Essential Rumi* on the shelves of the (heathen) friend I'm staying with that Thanksgiving. No *Essential Rumi* at The Bookloft by the Price Chopper in town. So I'm wondering if it should not in fact be called the *Inessential Rumi*, or the *Once Essential, but These Days Less So, Rumi*, as I walk empty-handed into Fuel on Main Street for the latte.

At least I can't fuck up a latte. Not in a coffee shop. That's what I figure. So I order for Dennis, and the barista responds:

"What size?"

Step two in a Recipe for Disaster when going to visit a dying god-relation: Not knowing how much coffee is appropriate to buy a dying man.

"Is it true a large latte is essentially a cappuccino? Confidentially? I knew a barista once who told me confidentially that he made lattes, cappuccinos, flat whites all the same. Never a complaint. That was Ohio, though, so."

That was me, stalling.

Blink. Blink.

That was the barista, blinking.

"One large latte, please." (Largesse, optimism, the gesture's all, I had Rumi bupkes.) "And a large red eye, for me." (If Dennis doesn't know what a red eye is, this will be something for us to talk about besides *The Elizabethan World Picture.* Coffee, add a shot of espresso.)

"Will that be all?"

"Also one large matcha almond latte." (Yes! Now I've got momentum! Maybe Dennis would like to try one if he hasn't yet—antioxidants! [Sure, bit late.] But also yummy when not too sweet; more chat fodder, that's where my head's at!)

And when the hot drinks arrive in their caddy and I've crested an unexpectedly cruel, rolling wave of tummy turbulence born from last night's ill-considered "why not?" dabble in Drambuie, Attila the Barista asks, "And what about something sweet?"

I pray for peace, consign my guts to God, approximate the true barista in my doubled vision, and touché ostentatiously: "I'm interested in your pumpkin spice donut. Yes, that vegan one."

Step three in a Recipe for Disaster when going to visit a dying godrelation: Get left alone.

Dennis is sitting at the head of the dining table. There are huge windows with crazy views of Mount Greylock.

I introduce the contents of my drink caddy.

He says, "I'll take the matcha."

Tina takes the latte, I my red eye. I pretend to forget the donut.

Dennis is tallow skinned, sitting upright, definitely riding an ebb-and-flow clarity. I can't imagine him eating a solid, even a vegan one.

There's a copy of *The Elizabethan World Picture* on the table, as well as a small press copy of Dennis's own poetry collection titled *White Flash*.

I ask him about his poems; he answers:

"Yes. This is . . ."

Tina and I sit in the pause for maybe nine Mississippis before Tina goes, not totally patiently, "The what, the what, Dennis, because we're just sitting here waiting for you to say the what, but if you don't know what the what is, you shouldn't make us wait for it."

These pauses and prompts are repeated a number of times, we lurch and languish, and then Dennis points out a black cat on the lawn that isn't there, and Tina announces she's off to the gym, and I'm suddenly left alone with Dennis. We regard each other, two dubious sous chefs in search of a special.

(At this point it occurs to me I'm not 100 percent sure *why* Dennis *is* my godfather. Tina and my mother had started a theater company in the Berkshires in the late seventies, and Dennis was kind of the rhythm section to the band—Charlie Watts to Mom and Tina's Keith and Mick. He was a devoted teacher, had been a Jesuit priest, played an exceptional Lear, but I was hard-pressed to find any standout memories of the man from my youth, besides a birthday when he bought me a skateboard and a pair of trendy Jams floral shorts. And, frankly, what's the purpose *of* a godfather to a forty-two-year-old divorced father of two [this is me], who admittedly grew up without an actual father? Why the lattes? Why the visit? Why this donut? Can someone in hospice for Parkinson's as well as prostate cancer [talk about excess]—can they still stomach solids, much less sweet solids?)

I tell Dennis how I meant to bring him Rumi, and he says he has a copy downstairs and stands up to get it.

He sways.

I really panic now because what if he falls? Is he allowed to use stairs? If I'm really honest, being alone with him, mainly I'm scared of him going to the bathroom not in the bathroom but instead in what he's wearing—so I ask if I can read one of his poems to him rather than the Rumi.

He remains standing, considers, and eventually says, "You could read me the second poem."

I open *White Flash* to its second poem and read its title:

"Remembering Sex."

Dennis sits. "It's been so long."

The poem is beautiful, erotic, positive—mouths open, bodies press, it glistens for maybe ten spare lines—and it's done.

"Would you like me to read the next one?"

"Which one is that?"

I tell him the title.

He says, "Hm, that's a good one." And when I finish and tell him the next title, he says, "You'll like that one." This goes on for about seven or eight poems, all of which are excellent, felt and heard, imagistic, personal, and plainspoken. After I've read him a quarter of the book, he asks me, "I was wondering, and I am aware that this may seem inappropriate on some level, if you would mind reading me the second poem again?"

So I read him "Remembering Sex" a second time.

It becomes clear as I read that while he admires the poems he's written about his times of torment—jealousies, self-loathings, and doubts—it's actually the poems about sex, about unities rather than disunities, that he wants to hear now, at the end.

Also a poem about his mother. I ask him what his mother did, and he says, "She was my mother." He smiles. I decide, finally, that it is time to hazard the donut.

"Would you like a donut now? I brought you a donut." I pull it out of its bag. The donut is brown and healthy looking, matte, grainy.

I break off a small bite-size chunk, like the size I would serve to my two-year-old. He looks at the little bite foggily, so I eat it, as if I've made it that size for myself. It's sweeter than it looks—not bad.

DONUT GO GENTLE

"It's pumpkin spice, they said."

Dennis says, "Mmmm," and reaches for the donut, stiff fingered. He begins to eat the solid. I am fairly confident at this point that he will live a few more months at least, well into the New Year—his skin is not so waxy or taut as I'd first thought. I watch him. I'm quiet. He eats and eats.

This is when Tina returns, and Dennis says, "I was hoping you'd come back, Teen, I've just been staring into space, and this guy's been staring into me."

Step four in a Recipe for Disaster when going to visit a dying god-relation: If you can't take the heat . . .

This kinda hurts my feelings, and I begin to wrap up my visit, but before I can get to the door, Tina says: "Wait. Dennis, did you tell Hamish the thing you wanted to say? Did you remember to tell him?"

Dennis doesn't open his eyes. "Yes. No. The main thing that I wanted to tell you, Hamish, is . . ." And he pauses again, but Tina doesn't interrupt this time. We hold, we hold, we hold, and then he leans in, sweeps the remaining crumbs of donut aside, lifts his almost empty cup of matcha, and whether this is the meaning of life or he has forgotten the question, Dennis's next word is "Cheers."

And we toast each other with paper cups.

And then Tina says, not totally patiently, "Yes, *but also*, you wanted to tell him how you pushed him in a stroller and took care of him *a lot* on West Seventeenth Street when he was just a baby. This was before we started the company, when he and your mum were such close friends, he was there for you when your mother was teaching, like a proper parent, mushing up your meals, that's why she made him your godfather, but there's no way you could remember that because you weren't even yet two. And now that you're grown, he wanted to see you once more and let you know."

Dennis smiled. "That too is true."

Step five in a Recipe for Disaster after visiting a dying god-relation: Let cool.

Tuesday morning, four days after the Friday after Thanksgiving, I wake up back in Los Angeles, check my phone, and see I have more texts than usual because Dennis has died during the night. And I'm stunned because I really thought he was going to live longer than four more days, because of how he looked and how he ate that donut.

But perhaps it was the season that had colored my judgment; perhaps this is what you expect at Thanksgiving, at the end of fall. That there will always be room for more. No matter the excess, no matter how full we are—another bottle will open, and the appetite will return.

FOOD AND LOVE ROLLED INTO ONE

 Sarah Jones

FOOD WAS MY FIRST REAL CRUSH.

Don't get me wrong, it had robust competition from the rambunctious, scruffy boys I began to notice as early as kindergarten during recess at school. But the only thing more compelling than daydreaming about which boy I wanted to sit with during lunch was *the lunch itself*. Didn't matter what it was. A tangy, pickle-y tuna sandwich, a crunchy PB&J washed down with whole milk, or, later, some cool-looking Lunchables-and-Capri-Sun combo cajoled out of a friend with more nutritionally lenient, free-spending parents than mine (at my house we had a code of whole-grain this and low-sugar that, no sleekly packaged brands). The prospect of mealtime thrilled me more than any boy could.

And this continued into my adolescence and adulthood. I found myself on dates with attractive men, but my eyes would wander from their gaze down to their plate of maple-glazed pork belly or truffled gnocchi or just some humble but divine fish tacos from a truck at three a.m. In fact, as much as I craved the kind of genuine, fulfilling relationships (whether romantic or with family and friends) I had always heard of and seen depicted in movies and on TV, something was very different for me. It felt as shameful as it was elusive and unnameable: there was an emptiness at my core, a longing for connection and love that I only seemed to be able to soothe with food. And so I lived among the normal people, my disordered eating mostly going undetected as I went to the movies largely focused on the popcorn and celebrated birthdays mainly waiting for everyone to leave so I could have more quality time with the cake.

As much as I thought I "loved to eat" and that deep down my grazing and bingeing were the closest surrogates I'd ever find for love, it became clear as I got older that even my most beloved treats had never actually sated my sense of separateness and unworthiness. Even two decades after college, I was still stuck in a cycle of attempted adulting through phases: plant based; all raw; paleo; "intuitive eating"; or whatever the latest slow/local/artisanal/macro buzzword was. No matter how I tried to manipulate and control my food, there was still an, ahem, all-consuming sense of loneliness and fear that paradoxically seemed to worsen with every bite I hoped would fix me.

One summer during a remote, serene island writers' retreat that should have felt like a highlight of my career, I was so obsessed with the sumptuous meals we were being served that I couldn't write a word. It was like my fears—of both failure and success—were somehow translating into an infinitely distracting hunger. That's when it hit me right between my food-fixated eyes: My real issue wasn't about eating at all.

It was about hiding and keeping myself small (at least metaphorically) by self-sabotaging, whether in relationships, in my creativity and career, or in anything else I pursued. I could finally see the truth about the voice that had always masqueraded as my protector by constantly reminding me that it wasn't safe to put myself out there. It was better to just eat because I wasn't good enough anyway—I was a fraud who was somehow born bad and wrong, and would always be less-than.

I now know I'm one of millions of people who have this kind of relationship with food, compulsive eating, and restricting/dieting to cope with deep emotional pain, crippling self-doubt—or even just day-to-day stress. I can also see in hindsight how much, in addition to having garden-variety food addiction, I was contending with other factors that reinforced my sense of less-than-ness. As a Black girl living a mixed-race experience (just walking around with my white-skinned mother and dark-brown-skinned father in the eighties and nineties made me want to stuff my face), being surrounded by racist, misogynist body-shaming disguised as "beauty standards" added layers (yep, there's a cake reference in there) to my unending sense of inadequacy.

That summer of the writers' retreat, I finally got help through a (free!!) disordered eating program and began to address my emotional dysfunction, which turned out to be the solution to my food problem. What I could not have anticipated was that it was also the comprehensive answer to the lack of love in my life. I don't mean that my getting "sober" from my food behaviors came along with a bonus boyfriend as part of the membership package. But I did begin to cultivate the kind of self-love I had only heard about (and snorted at) on treacly podcasts or the yoga retreats I'd occasionally attended (while bingeing my face off on their vegan buffets).

I learned, through really getting to know myself and accepting my imperfections, that the love I'd been seeking really, truly was within me all along. And while the fear that had ruled me didn't go away, it became something I could face and even triumph over, without needing to use a fork and knife as my only coping tools.

But that wasn't all. I also discovered that the (again, super-lame-sounding) premise of every (food-stained) self-help book that lined my shelves (mostly only half read) was also true: the way to attract love is by first becoming your own greatest resource for it instead of desperately grasping for it outside yourself.

And so it was that after several years of everything from journaling to inner-child work to affirmations, self-dates to solo vacations and even a self-honeymoon, as well as prioritizing my friendships and being of service to other people over how tight my abs were, I was so busy feeling like the cover of one of those self-help books that I let go of the hunt for the love match they promised.

I also cultivated a new relationship to food; while I could no longer treat it like a love interest, I also couldn't make it my sworn enemy. I had to stop trying to control it in any way, and instead *allow* it to become an enjoyable, balanced part of my life. Which is also how my partner ended up finding me and showing me how to let in more love than I'd ever previously known. Not by abandoning myself to cling to him, but by gradually learning what ingredients we were both bringing to the table, then incorporating them into a multilay-ered richness that balanced our collective flavors and nourished us both.

Metaphorically I'm speaking of our relationship, but I'm also describing a recipe we now prepare together that perfectly illustrates how love and food can combine in my life today, rolled into one. Whatever your eating habits, whatever your relationship status (including that all-important one with your true soul mate, yourself), I hope you'll try this recipe for tofu scramble breakfast burritos, which is plant based (but delicious enough to satisfy meat eaters).

Tofu Scramble Breakfast Burritos

INGREDIENTS

FOR SCRAMBLE:

- 1 package extra-firm organic tofu (frozen, then thawed)
- 1 large red onion
- 2 tablespoons tamari, divided
- 2 tablespoons brown rice vinegar, divided
- 1 tablespoon maple syrup
- 2 bell peppers (mix and match colors!)
- Scant tablespoon turmeric
- Twelve 10-inch flour tortillas (check to make sure there's no lard)
- Yellowbird Blue Agave Sriracha or other hot sauce, if you like your love on the spicy side 😉 (optional)

FOR REFRIED BEANS:

- One 16-ounce can vegan refried pinto beans (check to make sure there's no lard)
- ½ teaspoon cumin
- ½ teaspoon chipotle powder
- 2 cloves garlic, pressed
- 1 lime
- Pinch Maldon salt

FOR GUACAMOLE:

- 2 large ripe avocados
- Pinch Maldon salt
- ½ lime
- ½ tablespoon cold-pressed virgin olive oil
- Pinch cumin (optional)
- Pinch chipotle powder (optional)
- 1 onion, finely chopped, to taste (optional)

FOR PICO DE GALLO:

- 2 tomatoes, cubed
- Fresh cilantro, coarsely chopped, to taste
- Pinch Maldon salt
- Juice of ½ lime
- ½ tablespoon cold-pressed virgin olive oil
- Chipotle powder, to taste (optional)
- Cumin, to taste (optional)

FOR CHIPOTLE MAYO:

- 1 cup Follow Your Heart (see what we did there?) Vegenaise
- 1 tablespoon chipotle powder

TOFU SCRAMBLE

Please note: For this to work, you must freeze the tofu thoroughly and then let it thaw. I like to put the tofu in the freezer immediately after purchasing it, and then take it out the night before making the breakfast burritos. Freezing and thawing the tofu is one of the secrets to getting a fluffy, egg-like consistency. Freezing the tofu makes it recrystallize in such a way that once thawed, you can press all of the water out. This allows it to be light while still perfectly firm and ready to imbibe the flavors of the sauce.

Peel and cut the red onion in half, straight through the stem. Remove the remaining stem from each half. Then julienne the onion. I like to slice it from edge to center in thin slivers.

In a large cast-iron skillet on medium heat, pour roughly 1 tablespoon of tamari and 1 tablespoon of brown rice vinegar.

Sweat the onions for several minutes, then add roughly 1 tablespoon of maple syrup to gently caramelize them.

Meanwhile, cut the bell peppers in half down through the stems. Then cut thin, fajita-like strips lengthwise. Add these in once the onions are ready. Turn up the heat slightly to get a bit of a char on the blend of peppers and gently caramelized onions, then reduce the heat.

While this is underway, get started on the refried beans (see directions below).

Then cut open the tofu and divide it in half. Over the sink, grab one half at a time and press it between your hands as hard as you can, expelling all the water as if from a wet sponge.

Over the pan of simmering veggies, use your hands to grind and crumble each half of the tofu block into the mixture.

Now pour another tablespoon of brown rice vinegar and another tablespoon of tamari evenly over the tofu. Evenly dust it with slightly less than 1 tablespoon of turmeric, then stir the whole mixture thoroughly. The tofu should absorb the liquids and take on a yellowish, egg-like color from the turmeric.

Lower the heat to medium and stir regularly until any excess liquid has been absorbed or burned off. Then lower the heat and put a lid on to keep it warm.

REFRIED BEANS

Empty a can of vegan refried beans into a medium saucepan over medium-low heat.

Add half a teaspoon of cumin and half a teaspoon of chipotle powder.

Add a clove or two of peeled garlic, pressed.

Squeeze in lime juice to taste, for extra tang.

Add a generous pinch of Maldon salt.

Stir regularly and add just enough heat to keep warm.

GUACAMOLE

Halve and de-pit the avocados and empty into a small mixing bowl. With a fork, mash gently.

Add a pinch of Maldon salt.

Add the lime juice and half a tablespoon of cold-pressed virgin olive oil.

Optional: add a small pinch of chipotle and cumin; add very finely chopped onion to taste.

Gently combine.

PICO DE GALLO

Combine the tomatoes and cilantro in a small bowl.

Add a pinch of Maldon salt.

Press in the juice of half a lime.

Add half a tablespoon of cold-pressed virgin olive oil.

Optional: add a hint of chipotle and cumin.

Gently fold all ingredients together.

CHIPOTLE MAYO

Add a cup of Vegenaise to a small mixing bowl.

Add 1 tablespoon or more of chipotle powder.

Whisk until totally blended.

ROLL YOUR FOOD AND LOVE INTO ONE

Directly on an open gas flame, use tongs to warm the tortillas, flipping regularly.

Plate each tortilla, adding a large spoonful of the refried beans down the middle, from one edge to roughly three-quarters of the way across.

Now add a large spoonful of the tofu scramble, spreading it along the same line.

Next, add pico de gallo, guacamole, and chipotle mayo to taste.

Add hot sauce to taste.

Fold the bottom third of the tortilla lengthwise up over the ingredients, then fold in each side across.

You can also serve the pico de gallo, guacamole, and chipotle mayo separately to allow people to add to their taste.

THE SCAREDY BEAN

 Beanie Feldstein

I WAS LITERALLY AFRAID TO WRITE AN ESSAY FOR THIS BOOK.
Want to know why?

Because I am afraid of kitchens.

I'm sure you're thinking: Beanie, you can't seriously be afraid of a type of room that exists in every single dwelling around the world. You can't be afraid of "the heart of the home." You can't be afraid of the room that creates your favorite thing in the world—food.

Oh, but I *can.*

And so this might lead you to wonder: Beanie, did you have a terrifying or scarring experience that would lead to this fear?

No.

And so that might lead you to ponder: So, girl, what the hell is up?

And you know what, friend? I think the same exact thing. All the time.

So, let's get into it.

I am not afraid of sitting in kitchens or eating in kitchens. Therefore, it's not necessarily the physical space that I can't handle. It's the action that most people do when in kitchens . . . it's the cooking.

I'm scared of cooking.

The second my partner, Bon, starts cooking, which she does often and is quite good at, I shut down. I can't engage. Even now, as I type this, she is making a butternut squash soup, and truly the last thing I want to do on this planet is to participate.

Why?

I do not know. It's like a mental block. I see her go in there, and immediately all I want to do is anything else.

If I dig very deep and try to unpack it, I think it's because I'm afraid of getting it wrong. Or, more specifically, I'm afraid of getting it wrong to the point that it makes someone ill, or something horrific like that. It plagues me so deeply that it stops me from ever really trying. I dabbled in some light baking in my teen years, but since college and beyond I only ever make one single thing.

You see, I have only one friend in the kitchen: the egg.

You actually cannot cook an egg incorrectly. Trust me, I would know. The egg can be fried or poached or scrambled or boiled—there are so many ways to relatively get it right! And even if you don't get it right, it's not going to go disastrously wrong. It will just be "meh"! But it won't hurt anyone or anything! And if you really mess it up, you can always start over because there are more in the fridge. If I were to ever try cooking meat or fish (I wouldn't! Obviously!) it'd be so stressful—if you mess it up, there usually isn't another pound of salmon just there for you to try again. But the egg, the egg always has buddies left behind in the fridge. The egg is social! The egg travels in a pack!

So for all you scaredy pals like me out there who hate cooking but love eating, I offer you my recipe for a "meh" fried egg:

1. Get a pan, literally any pan.

2. Turn the stove on a heat, truly any level of heat.

3. Spray the pan with olive oil.

4. Crack one to three eggs, depending on your hunger level.

5. At a certain point, couldn't tell you when that point is, flip the eggs.

6. Eat.

MY TÍA, MS. ANA DOMINGA OTERO-SERRANO ROQUE'S, POLLO GUISADO!

 Rosie Perez

O KAY. SO THE LONG AND SHORT OF IT IS . . . I WAS LITER-
ally born out of drama on the high seas, a result of a dramatic
affair—scandalous, even. Yes, folks, I was a love child, as they
used to say. My father and mother were married to different people,
they met on a staircase in Brooklyn, went for coffee, and I happened.
They left their significant others but broke up a month before I arrived
and went back to their respective spouses with their tails between their
legs. Way back then, it was very scandalous to have a "bastard" child,
and when I was just a week old, to "save face," my birth mother ended
up giving me away to my father's sister, Ana Dominga Otero.

For the happy first few years of my childhood, I grew up believing that my aunt was my mother and my father was my uncle. As for my birth mother, I knew nothing of her. I was loved and spoiled like crazy. And boy did I love to eat. My favorite meal was pollo guisado with arroz blanco. That's Puerto Rican–style chicken stew with white rice. Yummy yummy! Happy times for sure.

Unfortunately, four years later my birth mother returned out of the blue and snatched me away from my aunt, only to place me in a Catholic children's home for unwanted, displaced, or orphaned children. Why? Who knows? Perhaps it was my birth mother's severe mental illness. Perhaps it was pain rife with jealousy. Either way, I was away from the only loving place I knew.

At the "Home" (that's what the kids and counselors called it), I was immediately told the truth. It was way too much for a small child to fully comprehend, yet I understood. On top of that, I was subjected to mental and physical abuse from the nuns. You know that old biblical belief "He that spareth his rod hateth his son: but he that loveth him chasteneth him betimes." Well, those nuns took it to new heights— they were brutal. I know! (By the way, when I saw the movie *Doubt*, I thought it was a dark comedy. Lol! But I digress.)

Anyway, I was miserable, to say the least. I went from being a happy-go-lucky, vivacious child who loved to show off, who danced and sang all the time, to an introverted, angry, shy little girl . . . who was still vivacious deep down inside and when the right time called for it. Oh yes, honey—as depressed as I was, they couldn't kill my shine completely. That part of me was never fully crushed. That's what four years of unconditional, good, healthy love and care does for a child. God bless America two times for that. And thank goodness I was still

MY TÍA, MS. ANA DOMINGA OTERO-SERRANO ROQUE'S, POLLO GUISADO!

85

able to go to my aunt Ana's house, who I affectionately called Tía, on weekends and holidays.

Because of the trauma, it would take me a day or two to return to my real self, and sometimes I'd never fully relax. When my Tía sensed that I was having a difficult time, she would always make me pollo guisado. The smell of the criollo Puerto Rican flavors would bring me right back to that happy place before my birth mother came and took me away. My Tía would set a bowl down in front of me and always follow it with the words "I love you . . . too much." Most of the time, I didn't reply back, couldn't reply back. It was just too much for my little soul to handle. Instead, I'd just smile and nod and dig in!

Years later, my Tía was able to get custody of me. It took a very long time for me to settle back into the only real home I knew. Everything just felt unsure, as if my mother would show up out of nowhere and take me away again. Although I didn't know it, I was suffering from full PTSD, depression, anxiety, and panic attacks. But once again, whenever Tía saw me like that, she would cook pollo guisado. The satisfaction with each bite let me know that I was safe. I was home and loved, once again.

Tía passed in 2001. I was devastated, but her spirit and love helped me through it. I have grown so much, especially when it comes to my mental health. I spent a lot of time and money to heal as much as possible. The PTSD really never goes away, and there are days when the depression hits hard. To help the blues go away, I remember Tía, pull out the big Dutch oven, and begin cooking. That same comforting feeling comes back each and every time I cook it for myself or my husband or family or friends. It just touches my heart in all the right and good places.

ROSIE PEREZ

Tía's Pollo Guisado

A few things to know about Puerto Rican cooking before starting.

Sofrito: With almost all traditional Puerto Rican cuisine, you must start with the base, which is sofrito. It's a mixture of certain vegetables and olive oil. You cook and use it like a roux. Puerto Rican–style sofrito doesn't usually use tomatoes, but other Latin Caribbean countries do. So do what you feel. I stick to my Tía's way without the tomatoes.

Achiote oil: Achiote is a Caribbean seed, a spice filled with flavor. We use it to color and season our oil. It comes in a paste form now, but I'm too old and don't know how much to use, so I stick with the seeds.

Adobo: Adobo is a mixture of garlic powder, salt, black pepper, oregano, and onion powder. Some people get fancy and add turmeric, cumin, and thyme. I like the old-fashioned kind. But that's just me. Plus, you get some of those other flavors with sazón (see below).

Sazón: Sazón's a seasoning mix of coriander, garlic, cumin, and annatto. Store-bought sazón has monosodium glutamate, or MSG, in it. MSG has gotten a bad name, but according to the FDA, it's pretty safe in moderation. You can make your own sazón or try hard to find one that is all natural. I use the store-bought kind. It's just easier, to be honest.

Okay! Let's start!

PREPARE THE SOFRITO

1 large green bell pepper, stemmed and seeded
1 large Spanish onion
½ pound ajíes dulces, stemmed and seeded
A couple of culantro leaves, not to be mistaken for cilantro
A few stems of cilantro
8 to 10 garlic cloves
Olive oil

Chop all the vegetables and add into a blender. Add just a bit of the olive oil and blend on low to medium. Slowly add more olive oil until you reach a mushy consistency. By the way, you can make more and freeze the rest. That's what real Ricans do. 😌 Set it aside.

PREPARE THE STEW STUFF—
THE CHICKEN AND VEGETABLES

3 pounds of chicken (thighs, breasts cut in half, wings) with the bones
    intact
Adobo seasoning
One 8-ounce can tomato sauce
2 or 3 big potatoes, quartered. Do not cut too small!
2 or 3 big, fat, long carrots, sliced somewhat thick on a diagonal
4 cups good chicken broth (or chicken bouillon)
½ cup Spanish green olive salad. It's a mixture of green olives, capers,
    and green olives stuffed with pimentos (you can get this at a store
    already prepared).
½ onion, sliced
½ red or yellow bell pepper, seeded and sliced
3 or 4 garlic cloves, slightly diced
¼ packet of sazón seasoning
½ cup chopped cilantro (optional)

Season the chicken with adobo pretty well, then set aside. Cut up your
vegetables. Set aside.

PREPARE THE ACHIOTE OIL

⅛ to ¼ cup vegetable oil
¼ cup achiote seeds

In a medium to large Dutch oven, pour just enough vegetable oil to cover the bottom of the pot, about ⅛ cup. Fire it up to medium-low. Add ¼ cup of achiote seeds and immediately turn the flame down to a low simmer.

Allow the oil to turn a burnt-red color, then let it cool just enough that you can strain the oil without burning the hell out of your mesh strainer. Throw the seeds away and return the seasoned oil back into the Dutch oven.

Now things get easier and a bit faster.

Turn up the heat to medium. Add the chicken and quickly brown, about 4 minutes on each side. Remove the chicken and set aside. Make sure you scrape up all the burned scraps from the chicken and stir them back into the oil. That's some good flavor right there!

On low heat, add about 2 to 3 heaping tablespoons of the sofrito and the whole 8-ounce can of tomato sauce to the achiote oil. Cook on low until brownish red.

Still on low heat, add the precooked chicken and all the juices from it, as well as the potatoes and carrots, to the pot. Stir until all are coated well. Quickly add just enough chicken broth that it almost covers the food. Then add the olive salad, sliced onions, red or yellow bell peppers, garlic, and ¼ packet of sazón, or to taste. Stir. Add more adobo to taste, only if needed. You want to taste the salt, but you don't want it to be too salty, so be careful!

Cover and bring to a boil. As soon as it boils, lower the heat to a simmer. Let it cook for about 20 to 30 minutes. Don't lift the lid until it's time! The potatoes and carrots should be soft enough that they cut easily. That's when you know it's done. Serve with cilantro, if using.

In the meantime, begin to prepare your white rice.

TÍA'S WHITE RICE

Short-grain white rice
Water
Vegetable or canola oil
Salt
One smashed garlic clove

THE TRICKS MY TÍA TAUGHT ME
ABOUT COOKING RICE

If you want the rice to be a bit firm, cook equal amounts of rice to equal amounts of water: one part rice to one part water.

If you like it more tender (NOT MUSHY! I HATE MUSHY RICE! WE DON'T DO MUSHY RICE! Sorry, had to get that out): one part rice to one and a half parts water.

Depending upon the amount of rice you make, cover the bottom of whatever size pot with vegetable oil. Not olive oil, but, like, canola oil. Heat on very low. Add your rice. I do about 2 coffee cups of rice. Make sure you coat all of the grains with the oil. Then, using the same coffee cup, add 2½ cups of water. Add about a teaspoon of salt. The water should taste just a bit salty, not too salty! Stir. Then add the smashed garlic on top. Do not stir. You already did that. Bring to a boil.

When you see that the water is absorbed to the point where it's about an inch or less above the rice, lower to the lowest flame possible. Cover and leave alone for 20 minutes. If the rice is too firm for you, add just a couple of sprinkles of water with your hand. If it's too mushy, God forbid, take the lid off and let it cook for 5 more minutes.

That's it! I hope it brings you and your loved ones as much joy and satisfaction as it always brings me.

To much love and good eating.

XO, Rose Perez

THE KARL-FASHIONED

 Kaley Cuoco

MMMM, I CAN TASTE IT NOW. MY MOUTH IS ACTUALLY watering. The smooth liquid coating my throat, the sting, the heat, the warmth, the way it makes you feel like you're floating . . . every single worry just floating away.

The truth is I wasn't always a bourbon drinker. I was an everything but bourbon drinker. It just wasn't my speed. I'd always been a wino at heart. A margarita or martini also always did the trick.

That is, until I met Karl. The meeting I'll save for another book at another time, but he was the one who introduced me to a whole new world. A world of bourbon.

On our first trip to Kentucky, he recommended we order a classic old-fashioned. I mean, duh, we were in bourbon country, so it felt like the right thing to do. We received our sparkly drinks in classic gorgeous tumblers, enriched with a perfectly cut single square of ice and a perfectly placed cherry floating on top.

We both took a sip.

It was good, but not great. We agreed it was way too sweet and something was missing. How could we make it better?

From that very moment, Karl was determined to create the perfect old-fashioned his way.

That's when the Karl-Fashioned was born.

This drink became a staple in our house and among our friends and family. If there was a gathering, everyone would make sure we brought the special ingredients for a Karl-Fashioned. During the holidays, Karl would set up our bar and there would be a legit line so everyone could get their special cocktail. It took forever because he made every drink by hand, and with love.

What made this drink oh-so-special?

Well, of course it started with a rye . . . he would then add a drop of scotch. Yes, that's right, scotch. This drink ain't for kids. . . . He then added a bit of Grand Marnier for sweetness (no simple syrup here) and five drops of bitters, and I'm not kidding, it had to be five drops *only*!

Then he would have me pick fresh oranges off our tree, cut them into gorgeous slices, and squeeze them right into the drink. Throw in a slice for good measure and overall presentation.

Oh, and we can't forget the ice!! You must have a large cube or a sphere. It's a rule!!

That's it. That's the Karl-Fashioned.

I can't tell you how many nights I would come home from an exhausting day at work and be greeted with this drink as I plopped on the couch. It was true joy. It made me smile. And it was Karl in a glass. Fresh, authentic, real, and made with love.

Sadly, this story doesn't end as happily as it started. Karl and I are no longer, and, I must admit, I haven't had a single Karl-Fashioned since we went our separate ways.

I can't get myself to do it. It doesn't feel right. That was our drink. Well, it was his drink. His creation. For us. And it always will be.

Before I wrote this, I asked Karl for permission to share his recipe. Of course he said yes, because that's who he is. A true gent. A man made of kindness and love. Just like that drink.

I hope you enjoy this cocktail the way I used to. With someone special. Cheers.

The Karl-Fashioned

Invented by Karl Cook. Enjoyed by Kaley Cuoco.

1½ ounces rye whiskey
¾ ounce Grand Marnier
½ to ¾ ounce scotch
5 drops bitters
Orange peel and a huge squeeze of fresh orange
Big ice cube

Enjoy.

A GOOD COOK IS HARD TO FIND

 Busy Philipps

I AM NOT WHAT ANYONE HAS EVER CALLED A *NATURAL* IN THE kitchen. Never have been. When I was a kid, my go-to after-school snack was made by placing tortilla chips on a plate, covering said chips with two slices of American cheese (Kraft Singles, let's not kid ourselves), and zapping it in the microwave for forty-five seconds. My mom worked as a real estate agent in Scottsdale, Arizona, where I grew up, and while her schedule was flexible, by the time I was in fifth or sixth grade, most afternoons I would walk home from the bus, let myself into our house, zap my nachos, and settle in for my favorite combination of after-school TV—*Oprah* and *Saved by the Bell*. Something about Oprah talking to me while I sat safely in my living room alone (at least until my sister got home from high school and commandeered the remote) and eating gooey, plasticky cheese on chips made me feel most . . . myself. It's no wonder that as an adult, when I'm in need of soothing I'll order nachos. In the year I was producing and putting up my late-night talk show *Busy Tonight* (RIP), I probably ate nachos, *no joke,* at least four times a week for dinner. And I almost *always* get nachos after a late therapy session. Therapy ends at six p.m. this week? No problem—I'll head straight to the nachos after, thank you.

I come by my uselessness in the kitchen honestly. My mother's own cooking prowess extended as far as the recipes she had been making since the early days of her marriage to my father—recipes that feel ripped out of *Better Homes and Gardens* circa 1965: beef stroganoff over egg noodles; tuna noodle casserole; chicken à la king; something she called *un*stuffed green peppers because, as she puts it, "I don't like stuffing them—it's too hard, Busy, they always fall over. It makes more sense to cut them up and lie them down *so that's what I do!*"; and spaghetti with meat sauce, which is ground beef cooked in the microwave plus a jar of Newman's Own Sockarooni sauce.

Oh, you didn't know you can cook ground beef in the microwave? My mom will cook *anything* in the microwave. Most of my mother's cooking took place in the microwave. Scrambled eggs? Microwave. Bacon? Microwave. Frozen pizza? MICROWAVE! Most of the vegetables I was served growing up were frozen and "zapped," with few exceptions. One such exception was certain casseroles (though some casseroles *could* be cooked in the microwave). My sister recently called our family a "casserole family," which made me laugh until I had to seriously consider how many cans of mushroom soup I probably consumed between the ages of two and eighteen. As my sister and I talked more, I realized we weren't just a casserole family growing up. We were the rare hyphenate "casserole–fast food family." It was similarly upsetting for me to think about the sheer number of Happy Meals I ate in my childhood.

Hundreds? Thousands?! Is that possible? I don't know. What I do know is that there's long been a story in my family that I was so enamored with McDonald's as a toddler that any time my mom's car pulled up to a stop—*any stop*—I would turn my head and yell out the window, "HAMBUGER FAAFAA PLEAAAA!" which was my toddler speak for "cheeseburger and French fries, please." Toddler me clearly assumed a Happy Meal would magically appear through the window when the car stopped if I asked for it because I *had seen it happen so many times*. I had a larger collection of Happy Meal toys and glassware than any kid I knew. Mostly because no one I knew was allowed to eat McDonald's as many times a week as we were.

The other exceptions to my mom's microwave rule were waffles on Sunday mornings cooked in the old waffle iron given to her by her mother, and the iceberg lettuce salads for dinner that at some point I became in charge of making, and which became my famous "garbage salads" that I *still* make when I'm home visiting my family to this day: iceberg lettuce, a can of black olives (drained, obviously), and whatever random lone vegetables I can find in the fridge—usually there's at least one tomato or a green pepper; occasionally there are some old baby carrots I can chop up and throw in, and if there are croutons in the pantry, I'll throw those in too. Add Newman's Own red wine vinaigrette, and *that's a garbage salad.*

By contrast, my best friend since I was five, Emily BB, had a mom and a dad who both loved cooking and cooked meals *from scratch* every single night for dinner, even though, like my parents, they both worked. Meals that seemed downright *exotic* to little me: A whole roast chicken over root vegetables? Orange roughy and potatoes that didn't start out as flakes?! Homemade *soup*? *You can make your own soup?* Even the pizza they ate was homemade. I rarely saw recipes being used. Emily's mom and dad seemed to just *make it up*. Also, Emily's family drank *water* at dinner. At my house you had two choices: 2 percent milk or Coke. I loved being at Emily's house for dinnertime, watching her mom expertly chop up onions and spices and add them to simmering pots. I always tried to play it cool when Emily's dad would say with a laugh, "Biz, you staying for dinner?" but I'm fairly certain they always knew what my answer would be.

By the time I got to high school, with my sister away at college and my dad traveling most weeks for work, my mother basically decided that she was done cooking altogether, and we ordered in 95 percent of our meals or went out.

My first years as a young adult living on my own in Los Angeles were culinarily lacking, *to say the least*. I had no idea how or what to cook or even how to grocery shop for anything that wasn't in the frozen section and ready to be microwaved and immediately consumed. Luckily (I guess), I lived on campus my first two years of college and therefore didn't have to worry about actually cooking food for myself. That's not to say I was making good or interesting choices; I was making predictably terrible choices—as in soft serve for breakfast kind of terrible. At some point freshman year, my roommate Diana and I realized we could use our campus dining points (the way our parents paid for our meals) at certain fast-food restaurants and pizza places nearby, which didn't exactly encourage either one of us to branch out food-wise. To save money (points), D and I would often order two pizzas on two-for-one day and then proceed to eat one whole pizza each, but we'd try to stretch it out over the whole next day so that the pizza was our lunch, snack, *and* dinner (and sometimes breakfast the next day, depending on whether or not we got stoned the night before). One particularly disgusting and memorable day, Diana and I bought *twelve* thirty-nine-cent cheeseburgers from McDonald's (I believe that was the limit allowed) to keep in our mini fridge so that for the next few days, whenever we got hungry, we could just zap one in the microwave. You know, how things get cooked!

The summer I turned twenty, my college friends and I all moved into an apartment off campus together, even though I wouldn't be returning to school in the fall because the TV pilot I had done was picked up and I was *officially a working actor*. My meals, however, still mostly came in a box, were frozen, or were delivered. The TV show I was on was *Freaks and Geeks*, and not only was it an incredible show, launching the careers of blah blah blah, but *most* important, it also happens to be where Linda Cardellini introduced me to the *breakfast burrito*. It might seem like a small thing, but for a kid from a casserole family, eggs in a burrito were unheard-of. That catering breakfast burrito *blew my mind*.

I would say for sure that my tastes expanded with every new acting job I landed in my early twenties: On a random made-for-MTV movie I was in (yes, MTV made movies for a minute—don't ask), one of the actors on set took me out to *real* ramen in Canada. During the filming of the movie *White Chicks*, the Wayans brothers taught me how to order amazing sushi (I had never had it!). Also on *White Chicks*, actor Jessica Cauffiel not only introduced me to Indian food but took the time to literally explain to me what everything on the menu was. SAAG PANEER 4 LYFE! And on *Dawson's Creek*, Michelle Williams and I forged our friendship partially (mostly?) over great wine, which she knew not only how to order but also what characteristics made for *good* wine. The wine I had been buying previously was generally Two Buck Chuck from Trader Joe's.

So, yes, thanks to *Hollywood*, my palate was expanded beyond the fast food it had grown up on! But *did I ever learn to cook*?! Well. Yes. I actually *did* learn to cook from Emily BB. My childhood BFF moved to Los Angeles after she graduated from Wesleyan to work in advertising, and she was my roommate from ages twenty-one to twenty-five. As she is her parents' daughter, she not only knew how to cook and grocery shop but *insisted* we cook our meals ourselves and eat at home. She also hated microwaves on principle and said we *shouldn't even have one in our home*. I won that battle, but Emily made me promise it would be used only as a last resort.

I was twenty-one years old. It was time: I had to branch out from fast food and garbage salads. Emily taught me how to roast vegetables in the oven, why mayonnaise was preferable to Miracle Whip, how to pick a good avocado at the farmers market, and how to properly season things—even salad! She showed me how to chop onions and use ginger and garlic (I know, I *know*, but trust me when I tell you I don't think my mother has ever purchased a clove of garlic in her life). Sure, my preferred appliance in those days was my George Foreman grill, but I was making *turkey burgers* at home! And grilled chicken salads! *Soup* not from a can! Eggs on the stove!

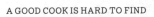

A GOOD COOK IS HARD TO FIND

99

I also started to experiment with cake decorating by making our friends fairly creative and intricately decorated cakes—one skill in the kitchen that I *did* pick up from my mother. My mom took a Wilton cake-decorating class shortly after she and my dad were married, and while he was in the navy. He would go out on nuclear submarines for weeks at a time, and my mother thought she might as well pick up a new skill while he was out at sea. This was long before my sister and I were even a thought to her, but she really took to the classes, and by the time my sister was born, my mom could have literally taught her own cake-decorating classes. Each year, a few days before my birthday, I would get so excited to see her Tupperware cake-decorating kit packed full of wax-lined pastry bags and Wilton tips and gel food coloring that were already older than I was by more than a decade come down from the highest shelf in the pantry. This was in the eighties and nineties, long before reality baking shows made whimsical cakes feel downright pedestrian. My mother once made a cake in the shape of a moose for my sister. A giant cheeseburger cake for my twelfth birthday. A clown cake. A cake shaped like Big Bird. They looked professionally done because our mom had a real talent for it, and the cakes always tasted amazing because "Betty Crocker knows what she's doing, Busy!" Yes, even our impressive homemade birthday cakes came from a box. (I do have to say, I'm actually with my mom on this one. Boxed cake mixes are generally better than scratch. Feel free to fight me on it. You won't win.)

Anyway, as the years of our rooming together went on, Emily and I would eat the occasional meal out, but when I wasn't working on a show, the shopping and daily meal planning became my job while Emily was working at her "real job." Most days, I would call Emily on her work line midday and we would discuss dinner so I could be sure to get all the requisite ingredients for that evening's meal. And then I cooked every single day. I got good at it! I could cook! Without recipes or canned soup! Emily and I ate at the black metal dinette set from my childhood that my parents had gifted me when I moved into that first apartment with my college friends most nights, which moved with me into my *real* apartment with Em (where I had the round upholstered seats re-covered from the original silver splatter-painted cushions reupholstered to a peach corduroy fabric I had found on sale). Some nights, we would eat in front of our TV, you know, if there was a new episode of something special like *Lost* or *Grey's Anatomy* on. But the food was cooked by us. Delicious and not from a box or the freezer, and rarely from a delivery person. Meals made from scratch. And that's how I've lived ever since. Forever and ever. The end.

No. Not really. But you knew that. Because you're very smart. Because you know you can't stay twenty-five and cooking meals with your childhood best friend in an upper duplex unit adjacent to Hancock Park forever. That's not what people do. People grow older and meet other people who they want to have children with and then marry those people and move in with them and have the children. People, like it or not, in one way or another, eventually turn into their parents.

Because as smart as you think you are, no matter how much money and time you sink into therapy unpacking your "family of origin"— your "casserole–fast food family," as it were—as far away from your hometown as you might move, one day you *will* (if you're me) find yourself in a kitchen, making nonorganic Kraft mac and cheese *in a microwave* for one of your precious children whilst simultaneously tracking on your phone your other precious child's Postmates order from

Taco Bell *and* your own Uber Eats order from the gluten-free pizza place you love, and you will think or possibly even say out loud to no one in particular, "Good lord. How in the hell did *this* happen?"

The truth is, like most things in life, like perhaps maybe *life itself*, it just sneaks the fuck up on you. It's said that each generation is supposed to be a bit better off than their parents', right? Look, I'm aware that, *historically speaking*, the powers that be who write about rising or falling generational U.S. living standards (economic strategists? sociologists? Malcolm Gladwell?) probably weren't really talking about how people today feed their children food cooked in the microwave and fast food *less often* than their parents did, but who's to say that it's not quantifiable progress?

The choices we make are ours and not our parents', to be sure. I've done enough good therapy to know that. But maybe, *maybe*, some of the pathways are grooved so deeply that certain things may just be unavoidable eventualities. Maybe a hankering for McDonald's is passed down somehow in our DNA like generational trauma because, I swear to God, I don't even *know* how my children knew they would love it, but they did and they do. *They just do.*

Yes, shopping and making home-cooked meals every day for my BFF and myself at age twenty-three was fun and gave me a plan for the day, especially when the only other plan I had was to binge-watch *Law & Order: SVU* in a midday marathon and figure out what DNA I'd leave for Stabler to find if I got snatched while walking the dog later (fingernails).

But now I'm forty-two years old and somehow have more jobs than I know what to do with, all demanding a ton of attention—including my actual favorite and the hardest job of all time, being the mom to two brilliant kids, who are now thirteen and eight.

Just like my mother before me, I'm not a mom who roasts a chicken every night, unless if by *chicken* you mean frozen nuggets, and by *roasts* you mean seven minutes in the air fryer (which I declare the *microwave of our generation*). But you know what? I do make a whole chicken for them sometimes. Once. One time I did. I also made both kids homemade baby food from organic farmers market fruits and veggies in a special baby food steamer/processor thing (with the help of their full-time nanny, Iliana). My kids eat salmon rice bowls and black beans (again, thanks to Iliana) and love the farmers market and know how to pick the perfect avocado (thanks to their dad). I have never once made them a meal where the base is a can of mushroom soup. I've watched as the kids learned how to make fresh pasta with their dad, and I've shown both of them how to make my grandmother's waffle recipe.

Try as we might, it's not easy to escape the patterns of one's childhood. We all do the best we can. Some days are better than others. But some weeks, I just don't have it in me, and so I find myself giving in to the repeated calls for "Hambuger faafaa pleaaaa!" But without question, every year on my kids' respective birthdays, *my* Tupperware cake-decorating kit comes out of the pantry, and Betty Crocker and I make those kids the cake of their damn dreams.

MY MORNING RITUAL

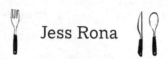

Jess Rona

N O MATTER HOW BUSY I AM, I MAKE SURE TO DO THIS tiny thing for myself every morning.

Coffee

There's really nothing like it, if you think about it. That first sip of hot, bitter, sweet comfort is the one thing I look forward to every single morning besides carrying my chubby poodle, Meemu, from our cozy bed to the backyard to go potty. An incredibly satisfying cup of coffee in the morning has been the number-one most consistent thing in my life for decades.

My coffee adventures started when I took a coffee-roasting class at this place in Altadena called the Institute of Domestic Technology. I could not believe how easy it was to roast coffee beans! That said, I am way too busy these days to do anything like that. As a small business owner, I work so much I can barely feed myself (don't worry, I eat . . . ooh baby, I eat).

I've had fancy twenty-dollar bags of coffee and less-fancy five-dollar bags. It's all wonderful. However, the fancy shit is extremely delicious. Also, it feels fun to treat yourself to something nice, and I'm all about feeling good these days. So go ahead and get some. You deserve it, you legend.

Milk

Back in the day, before my small business felt like I had ten babies, I loved food crafting. I still do! I made kombucha, took culinary classes, tinkered with new recipes, and made nut milks.

But whoaa baby. These days I have lots of plates spinning. I am the owner of Jess Rona Grooming—the best dog-grooming shop in all of Los Angeles. I have a book, merch, employees, a show on HBO Max (*Haute Dog*), and I'm launching a product line. . . . It's madness.

Because my life is bonkers, I created a quick and easy way to make nut milk in five minutes, minus a little bit of prep, that I still use all the time. So if you're a busy bee like me, you can do it too. When you're feeling fancy, I encourage you to try my nut milk creamer recipe and add it to your coffee. It's a tiny way to spend a little extra time being shmoopy with yourself.

Sugar

I know how important a perfect cup of coffee is, so sweeten as you like. I'm not going to tell you how to live your life. Take it sweet, take it black, take it with you on a hike (just kidding—I have no idea how people hike with hot coffee in their hands, but people are loons in my town).

There was a time when I was all about stevia, then I moved on to coconut sugar, and now I'm a honey girl. I love my coffee semisweet and creamy with a bitter finish. *chef's kiss*

So now . . . I'd like to present to you . . .

A tiny man and an orchestra pop out of the floor with top hats and jazz hands

My Morning Ritual

Treat yourself to a gift for your senses. A slow, fancy pour-over heaven. You won't regret it. And I added a tiny spiritual practice too, just in case you're in the mood to give your divine self a high five.

SUPPLIES

FOR THE COFFEE:

Kitchen scale (I got one for $11 on Amazon.)
Chemex
Coffee filter for pour-over
Gooseneck kettle (A regular kettle works too, but it's not as precise of a pour.)

FOR THE NUT MILK CREAMER:

Vitamix blender (or other high-powered blender)
Nut-milk bag (I got mine for $9 on Amazon.)
Big-ass bowl
Hot water

FOR THE SPIRITUAL PART:

Journal
Pen
Love in your heart

INGREDIENTS

FOR THE COFFEE:

Freshly ground coffee that's medium-coarse grind for pour-over

FOR THE NUT MILK:

Cashews or almonds
Shredded coconut
Dates (optional)
Sea salt
Vanilla extract (optional)

COFFEE RECIPE (FOR ONE CUP)

Heat kettle to 195°F to 205°F.

Place filter so the three folds are flat over the pour spout, and rinse filter with hot water (this will heat up the Chemex and seal the filter in place).

Dump out the hot water (in the sink, silly!).

Add .7 ounces (20 grams) of coffee, and then tare the scale back to 0.

Pour hot water over the grounds just to fully wet them, and then allow the coffee to bloom and expand. Pure joy. *If your scale has a timer, press start as you do the first pour (the whole process should take about 3 minutes).

Wait 30 seconds.

Gently pour hot water over the grounds in a circular motion bit by bit until you reach 10.58 ounces (300 grams).

Celebrate.

NUT MILK CREAMER RECIPE

For bulk-batch creation: At least 8 hours before you want your nut milk, take 4 to 8 cups of cashews or almonds, put them in a big-ass bowl or jar, and cover with filtered water. Allow to soak for 8 hours or more.

Strain and rinse well.

Add them to a plastic ziplock bag or some kind of freezer bag and put it in the freezer. Now you have soaked nuts for whenever you want to make nut milk.

Add 1 to 2 cups of nuts, ½ cup of shredded coconut (and dates, if you want) to a blender.

Cover with hot water and let it sit for a few minutes to break down a bit.

Add about 2 cups of water (the less water, the thicker it'll be—play with it).

Blend like a lunatic.

Get your big-ass bowl, put your nut milk bag in it, and pour the mixture through.

Seal the bag and squeeze (it helps if you tighten your abs and think about how much you love your dog).

After you strain the nut milk, add a pinch of sea salt and vanilla into the milk, if you like.

Pour the milk into a cute little jar.

Celebrate.

Add your creamer and whatever sweetener you like to the coffee, and sip as you follow these prompts in a journal/notebook:

This is inspired by one of my favorite books of all time, The Magic, *by Rhonda Byrne.*

- **Write out five things you are grateful for and why.**

- **Read through them, close your eyes, and say thank you to Source/the Universe/God.**

- **Inhale and feel gratitude flow through you.**

I am grateful for _____ *because* _____. *Thank you.*

Do this every morning and watch your life evolve in glorious ways.

xoxo,

Jess

INTUITIVE EATING

 Sian Clifford

ONE OF MY FAVORITE SCENES FROM THE FILM *HOOK* IS when Peter—played by the late, great Robin Williams—gathers with the Lost Boys around the table, waiting for dinner. In the midst of the giddy chatter and excitement, a stream of steaming platters pour out of the kitchen, and following an obligatory choral squall of "GRACE!" the boys launch themselves at the food as though it were the most delicious and decadent feast you could ever dream of. But Peter is looking at nothing. The boys' hungry hands and mouths are grappling with air, the plates and dishes sit empty. It's only once Peter is goaded into a bout of insults with Rufio, the boys' unrivaled leader, flicking his spoon at Rufio and landing a mass of fluorescent mush onto the boy's mortified face, does the boys' banquet finally reveal its magnificent glory before him. He hasn't been able to see it up until that moment because he's forgotten who he is. He's forgotten to use his imagination.

My formative memories of food can all be found in movies or books or while I was bustling around my mother's legs in the kitchen on Sundays. Whether it's sausages sizzling in *Danny the Champion of the World*, multicolored never-ending Gobstoppers in *Willy Wonka & the Chocolate Factory*, ice cream feasts in *Home Alone*, Butterbeer in Harry Potter, or roast dinners and apple crumble in my own mother's kitchen, they all evoke the same feelings for me: joy, ritual, comfort, nourishment, connectedness, and, perhaps most significantly, deep, truly scrumptious satisfaction. They are the innocent feelings of a child before she forgot who she was and her relationship to food changed forever.

The story of when and how that happened is quite simple. It features all the usual suspects, some of the greatest hits including but not limited to: relentless comments about my appearance and my weight for as long as I can remember—being too thin, not being thin enough; surrounded by women perpetually on diets, restricting their food, bingeing on food; the incessant discourse between superfoods and super-super-duper foods; the endless daily bombardment from magazines, commercials, toys, and normalized popular culture all sending out grossly mixed messages on how to look, who to be, and where in that given moment one fell on a scale of nowhere near to not quite perfect.

I was complicit in a series of silent cultural pacts. Accepting of a subliminally sourced standard of beauty that I neither understood nor could ever seem to attain, so mercurial was it in its nature. Attributing an overwhelming unspoken untruth as a universally accepted fact, that thinness equals radiant health. Oh, and joy. Of course. Always joy. What did someone famous allegedly say? "Nothing tastes as good as skinny feels."

Wading beyond and dragging myself out of the psychological quagmire of those adopted mindsets and misbehaviors has been such a gradual, messy, and challenging journey, it's almost impossible to isolate the specific footholds that eventually levered me to safety. But the place I have arrived at now, while being incredibly personal in its discovery, is, I genuinely believe, universal in its sublime joyfulness and the ease with which you can experience true radiant health.

Somewhere, I'm not sure where but let's say around midway, clawing my way out of the swamp, I stopped passively consuming media—magazines, the socials, fad diets, what worked for someone else, what worked for everyone else, what's good, what's bad, what's the latest kind of body beautiful—and started listening. At first amid the clamor of fading social commentary and my own ever-critical inner dialogue, it was incredibly hard to hear anything at all. But I could feel.

I started to recognize that my body craved what it needed and craved the source that would fulfill that need the quickest. I noticed that even when just thinking about certain foods, my body would experience an incredibly subtle feeling of expansion if it felt good, and a contraction if it didn't. At the time, I was curious and exhausted enough to see what might happen if I were to trust those signals and surrender to them entirely.

Suddenly, I stopped seeing cravings as the enemy—they were simply communications from my body to tell me what it required in that moment. It was up to me to select the food source to meet those desires, of course, though I discovered that my body wasn't fussy at all, even if I was. I experienced a dawning realization that up until that point, I saw all food through a terrifying kaleidoscopic filter of good and bad, right and wrong, learned and made up. Food had become something alien, something separate from me that I had to analyze and monitor at all times, like it was something to be suspicious of. Sometimes I couldn't even tell if I was hungry or thirsty. It was completely overwhelming. Thankfully, my intuition, incrementally building in confidence and volume, had my ear and convinced me to keep going. So I kept listening. Kept tuning in. Kept trusting. And slowly, slowly, ever slowly . . . I remembered.

I remembered those feelings of joy, ritual, comfort, nourishment, connectedness, and deep, truly scrumptious satisfaction. The way I'd felt about and enjoyed food before the world, diet culture, and sometimes even my loved ones, got in the way. Then I had another epiphany—I remembered being bent double in pain when eating some stomach-spasming dairy. I'd not only ignored this at the time but muted it and kept going. Even when my body was protesting desperately and not being the least bit subtle at all, I had silenced myself. It was me. No wonder I was struggling to hear what it had to say now—I had cut off the lines of communication.

I began to realize that this extraordinary part of my nature had the power to bring me back to who I really am. A source of intelligence so inexhaustible that no matter how much I tried to pretend it didn't exist, it had just sat back waiting quietly, patiently, until I was ready to turn down the volume on the cultural dialogue and listen. Really listen. To the most assured, nuanced, perfect guidance for my body and its completely individual needs. I believe each of us has this power residing inside of us. It could not care less about shape or size. Its sole desire is for our supremely unique, optimum well-being. It contains a well of knowledge beyond our comprehension. A language we've forgotten we're fluent in.

All I look for now when I'm eating is a resounding internal "yes." It doesn't matter if it's a green juice or a chocolate bar, if it worked for my friend or if it didn't, or even if my body said "no" to the same mealtime query yesterday—I just ask the question and respond accordingly in that given moment. No restrictions, no micronutrients, no weighing scales, no guilt. I acknowledge, respect, and prioritize my body's decisive knowing and trust that it knows better than I do. That it is communicating with me at all times and always has—if I'd only care to listen.

Since making this shift within myself from the inside out, my health, my joy, and my relationship to my body have all flourished. I recognize all food as food, neither good nor bad. I trust that our inner guidance systems have the capacity to work out the rest.

Intuitive eating is about listening and acceptance.

It's using your imagination.

It's sensory memory and perception.

It's freedom.

It's trust.

It's Bangarang.

Out beyond ideas of wrongdoing and rightdoing, there is a scrumptious feast—I'll meet you there.

Chocolate Mousse

My body generally says no to dairy and sugar, but you can sub in double cream for the coconut milk and 1 teaspoon of golden caster sugar for the maple syrup if that feels good to you.

Prep time: 5 minutes (not including soaking or setting time!)
Cooking time: 0 minutes

MOUSSE

One 13.5-ounce (400-ml) can full-fat coconut milk
½ cup pitted dates (soaked in water for 1 to 2 hours, then drained)
⅓ to ½ cup cacao powder (to taste)
1 tablespoon maple syrup
Pinch of sea salt
Seeds from 1 vanilla bean (optional; equivalent to 1 tablespoon vanilla extract or 1 teaspoon vanilla essence)
Pinch of cinnamon (optional)

TOPPINGS—WHATEVER YOU FANCY!

SOME SUGGESTIONS:

Handful of raspberries
Pistachios
Pinch of sea salt
A drizzle of maple syrup

Place all the mousse ingredients into a good-quality blender or food processor with an S-blade in the order as written, and blend until well incorporated—scrape down the sides and stir in between, if necessary. Decant into small bowls or ramekin dishes, and place in the refrigerator for 1 to 2 hours until set and/or ready to serve. Before serving, sprinkle with desired toppings. Best eaten fresh but will keep without toppings for up to 3 months in the freezer.

PLANET HELEN

 Nikole Beckwith

M Y MOTHER'S MOTHER'S NAME WAS HELEN. DURING the bulk of my childhood, Helen worked at a fine-jewelry counter at Jordan Marsh in the Northshore Mall before it became Macy's. My mom worked at the fragrance counter of the same mall after transferring from the curtain department. Three of my mother's four sisters also worked at The Mall, making the tiled, brightly lit maze of glass cases and clothing racks an extension of home.

Helen, or Grandma, as we knew her, lived in a manufactured neighborhood called Northridge Properties, before it became Northridge Homes. Two of our aunts also lived there. From first through fourth grade, my sister and I spent most days after school at Northridge because when Helen or our mother wasn't at work, either Helen was watching us or my mother was watching our cousins. We trick-or-treated at Northridge, hunted for Easter eggs there, and the first penis we ever saw belonged to a neighbor boy who wanted to play doctor there. After seeing the penis, my sister and I ran away. Recounting the story to Helen, she advised us to do what she always advised us to do when confronted by something uncomfortable or unwanted: "Kick him in the shins." It was a formative place and a formative time.

When I was eleven and my sister was nine, we moved almost an hour away. Then my aunts moved, then my grandmother. Everyone stopped working at The Mall and we all saw less and less of one another. Much less once I started piercing things and breaking open Sharpie markers to dye my hair. By the time I finished rebelling and started settling into the blueprint of who I am now, Helen was sick. After waking from a coma, strokes and swelling around her brain had claimed her memory.

Just as I was finding my identity, she was losing hers.

Having never had the chance to truly know each other as people, my memories of her are mostly visceral: How it felt to pull her sliding-glass door open, grass-stained and sweaty from a game of tag, to slip into the cool, crisp quiet of her living room. Tracing the big cream flowers and winding green vines of her blue floral couch with my finger while she read to us. The way the glass of her coffee table would shake against its thick wood frame when we pressed down hard with our crayons. The texture of the carved nativity scene figures she would put out for Christmas, and her patience when we would animate them in the same kind of dramas our Barbies had at home. But more than anything, my memories of Helen are rooted in food.

Helen was a woman of routine and ritual. She would make Lipton black tea in a blue and white teapot served with milk, sugar, and Annas Swedish Thins—a crisp ginger cookie with petal edges and grains of sugar on top. The box opened like a jewelry box might and gave the cookie a very serious air. Her pocketbook (as she called it) always had

Dentyne gum inside—this was before gum had flavors with names like "Fire" and "Ice Arctic Chill." It came in one flavor (cinnamon) and has since been discontinued.

While Helen always had butterscotch and Starlight peppermint candies in her living room, I remember being most impressed with the Andes mints on a small dish in the middle of her dining table. At the time, Andes were fancy—the wrapper was metallic green with silver writing folded closed like a present. Proving their fanciness, the Andes were also harder to reach and more difficult to sneak; we had to get up on one of the chairs and stretch our torsos as far as they could go to get one, at which point Grandma would see us from the kitchen and we would try to pretend that stretching your torso across the table was super fun and had nothing to do with the Andes mints.

In the kitchen, Helen would be baking and making. Like many people, grandmothers especially, food was her love language. Helen raised eight children as a working single mother, something I would not understand the enormity of until we were already lost to each other. The kitchen was a place to care for and connect with her children, which continued into her children's adult lives and her relationships with their children. According to my mom, she also made bacon and eggs for the family dog in the morning. It was not only how she said "I love you"; it was how she said "I'm here."

In fall and winter, she made brownies, mincemeat pastries, and spice cakes. In summer, chocolate chip cookies and homemade strawberry shortcake—everything from scratch. In spring, she made a great red potato salad (we were a Miracle Whip family) and chicken pot pie. When making dinner, the rule was each meal had to include "two greens and a yellow"—beans, peas, and corn, for example.

Tomato soup and grilled cheese—both sides of the bread buttered—were staples. In fact, every sandwich was buttered, grilled or not. Helen believed butter was part of the essence of a sandwich, not a condiment. The butter went on regardless of any other spread—a given. It was not a "peanut butter *and butter* sandwich," it was a peanut butter sandwich. Mentioning the butter would be akin to mentioning the bread.

It wasn't any one thing she made that has stayed with me, not specific flavors or recipes; rather, it is the continuity and repetition of the whole picture. That kind of consistency made those foods an extension of her, the flora and fauna of Planet Helen—store-bought staples just as meaningful as the homemade meals. She is in the room whenever I have potato salad or make whipped cream, even if it's vegan (part of my rebellion that became part of my blueprint). I think of her every time a Starlight peppermint or an Andes mint comes with the check at a restaurant. As far as I am concerned, she invented all those things.

While we didn't get to turn the page to a new chapter of knowing each other as I got older, the chapter Helen and I had is still something I carry with me. While I was writing this, my mother reminded me that Helen never wore an apron when she cooked—her pants always ended the day dusted with flour. I flashed back to looking up at her in the kitchen as she handed me the mixing bowl and a teaspoon to lick clean, flour on her pants and a tea towel slung over her shoulder for her to wipe her hands on.

Six months ago I bought my first apron. Never worn, it hangs by my sink, and I dry my hands on it in passing after doing the dishes. My counter, however, is peppered with tea towels, flung from my shoulder where I keep them when I'm cooking, the front of my jeans dusted with (gluten-free) flour.

A SAD BUT DELICIOUS VEAL BLANQUETTE

 Kwame Onwuachi

I WAS NINETEEN YEARS OLD AND I HAD JUST DROPPED MY FIRST mixtape, so I felt it was only a matter of time until I had my big rap break. During the week I would wait tables, slice bread, and pour water at Tom Colicchio's restaurant Craft. "This is just temporary," I would say to myself. A means to an end toward music fame. Touring, BET, movie parts—those were all my destiny. Working in restaurants was a stepping-stone, but it was a large one, actually.

During the weekend I would perform at the Nuyorican Poets Cafe in Alphabet City. The concert was called "Music, Mingle, and Munch," and in between sets I would serve canapés. It was a lot of work, but I had to pay the rent. And that's where I met Jasmine.

I'm not sure I believe in love at first sight, but I was clearly infatuated with this girl. She was a friend of a friend and we quickly hit it off. Because I still had one foot in the kitchen, I figured, why not invite her over for a candlelit dinner cooked by yours truly? Hey, it worked in the movies, so I thought I would give it a shot. I invited her over to my place and she obliged.

At the time I was reading this book on culinary fundamentals, so I thought a nice veal blanquette would be perfect. I looked up a butcher in my area and got some veal shank as well as short ribs—I wanted to intensify the flavor. I also bought a nice bottle of white wine and made sure to deepen my voice so that the clerk wouldn't ID me. It worked. Next was the market for potatoes, Swiss chard, and mirepoix. I was so hyped to start cooking!

I got home and went straight to work with the sultry sound of Erykah Badu in the background. The scents started coming together. Searing the meat to get that beautiful crust, or Maillard reaction. Ricing the potatoes and emulsifying the cream and garlic into it. Reducing the wine, straining the sauce, oh my God, it was a symphony. By nine p.m. the meat was so tender you could cut it with a curse word. She was supposed to arrive at 9:15, so I cleaned up like my parents were in the driveway. Looked in the mirror one final time for a wave check, and then it was game time.

By 9:45, I knew what was up: she was a no-show. I texted her "thanks for standing me up" and threw my phone on the bed, then I sluggishly walked to the kitchen and made myself a plate. Normally you're not hungry after cooking, but I was sad, so I ate. And I ate. And I ate. It was delicious, and by the time I finished, I was actually laughing, kind of glad she hadn't made it because there was more for me. I thought to myself, *Maybe I should take this cooking thing seriously?* What a crazy idea, huh?

Years later I still make this dish, but now with a spin all across the world. This is an ode to the OG that helped spark a fruitful and delicious career.

Veal Blanquette with Mashed Potatoes

COMPONENTS

Veal Blanquette
Mashed potatoes (as desired)
½ bunch chives, chopped

METHOD

Spoon mashed potatoes on plate and top with hefty ladleful of veal blanquette.

Top with chives and enjoy!

VEAL BLANQUETTE:

- 2 sprigs thyme
- 3 garlic cloves
- 2 bay leaves
- 1½ pounds veal shank cut into 1½-inch cubes
- ¾ pound short ribs cut into 1½-inch cubes
- House spice (Creole) to taste
- Mustard, whole grain, as needed
- Salt to taste
- 1 tablespoon grapeseed oil
- 1 cup dry white wine
- 5 cups chicken stock
- 2 carrots, small diced
- 1½ onions, small diced
- 2 stalks celery, small diced
- 1½ tablespoons butter
- 1½ tablespoons flour
- 1 cup heavy cream
- 1 teaspoon lemon juice
- Freshly ground black pepper to taste
- Cayenne pepper to taste

METHOD

Add thyme, garlic, and bay leaves into a sachet, or wrap in cheesecloth and tie securely. Set aside.

Season veal and short ribs with Creole spice, mustard, and salt. Place 1 tablespoon of grapeseed oil in a Dutch oven and place on high heat. Sear the meat on all sides until golden brown, then remove from pan. In the same pan, add dry white wine, deglaze the bottom of the pan, and simmer until reduced by half. Add 5 cups of chicken stock to the pan and place the meat back in fully submerged, with the thyme, bay leaf, and garlic. Bring to a simmer and reduce to medium-low heat, removing all impurities that rise to the surface. Cook, covered, for 1 hour.

Add chopped carrots, onions, and celery, and cook until tender, about 20 minutes. During the last 15 minutes, place the flame on high to reduce the liquid to about half.

In another saucepan make the blond roux: melt butter, add flour, and cook until smooth. Stir constantly. Do not let brown.

Add the heavy cream and roux to the braised veal pot, stirring to incorporate. Bring to a simmer, then cook on medium heat until thickened, around 15 minutes.

Stir in lemon juice and season with salt, pepper, and cayenne pepper.

GARLIC MASHED POTATOES:

> 2 pounds Yukon Gold potatoes
> Water as needed
> Salt to taste
> 1 cup heavy cream
> 1 cup unsalted butter
> 3 garlic cloves

METHOD

Peel, chop, and place the potatoes in a saucepan, and cover with 1 inch of cold water; season generously with salt.

Bring pot to a boil, and cook until the potatoes are tender, about 20 minutes.

Add the heavy cream and butter into another pot and place over low heat.

Finely chop the garlic, or use a microplane to grate, and add to the heavy cream.

Allow heavy cream to warm up (do not let simmer).

Drain the potatoes and push them through a ricer (or food mill, tamis, or mash) into a bowl.

Add the garlic heavy cream little by little, using a spatula to fully incorporate the heavy cream into the riced potatoes.

Adjust the seasoning.

THE EVOLUTION OF A CHERRY TOMATO

 Kathryn Budig

I FEARED THE CHERRY TOMATO AS A CHILD.

And for good reason—or so I believed. They were, it seemed to me, reserved for adults in the same way that nectar and ambrosia were intended for the gods—beautiful in concept, but obviously lethal to a mere mortal child like myself. This reasoning, however, never held up in the Court of Mother, where all things were judged. She would roll her eyes at me, carefully transferring each captive tomato onto my plate at a painfully slow pace.

This was when I would launch into my second trusted argument: How, pray tell, was I supposed to eat a food that I couldn't properly spear with my fork? These little balls were like the sand crabs of vegetables (okay, okay, technically *fruits*, though they were horrid little vegetables to me), scattering at the first glimmer of a utensil. And rules were rules, so I couldn't swap my fork for a spoon or swoop in with my hands (this latter policy was a close second to the number-one dinner-table rule that I'm convinced applied only to me: no singing at the table). Every failed attempt to spear their bulbous bodies sent them shooting across my plate like a pinball.

But here's the real rub. Even though I abhorred the cherry tomato, I couldn't deny the truth: They were so damn *pretty*. And the adults who ate them looked so *sophisticated*. It clearly took an accomplished human to tame and successfully wield these wild beauties. Besides, didn't they fall into the fun-size category? Like Frosted Mini Wheats or baby Butterfingers, they *had* to be kid friendly, like *Honey, I Shrunk the Tomato*. Determined, I developed the Nestlé Technique (trademark pending). I'd usher the cherry tomato toward the deepest folds of my iceberg lettuce—classy choice of greens, I know—where I would hopefully dispose of its body, or, on brave days, skillfully slide my fork under the acidic land mine and lift it cautiously to my lips. I'd let the red orb careen into my mouth, where my teeth would clamp down, hopeful, and—*pop!* Tale as old as time—my eyes would bulge, unable to contain my physical reaction to the explosion of gelatinous tomato guts.

That was then.

This is now. And, oh—how things have changed.

I now pop cherry tomatoes like candy. I worship them—the breaking of their sweet skin after a long, hot bath of olive oil, salt, and chili pepper—and I would happily trade a

THE EVOLUTION OF A CHERRY TOMATO

bucket of popcorn for a carton of Sun Golds. (Please don't tell nine-year-old me.) That's right, I've become that "adult" I once watched with a blend of awe and disgust. But isn't that the beauty of the culinary experience? We age and grow, our tastes expanding from khaki-colored food groups covered in melted cheese to a rainbow of possibility. Which is why I hope you enjoy my lemony rice with Sun Gold tomatoes, lentils, and arugula—no Nestlé Technique necessary, and singing is absolutely welcome.

Lemony Rice with Sun Gold Tomatoes, Lentils, and Arugula

SERVES 4 TO 6

INGREDIENTS

1 large garlic clove
2 large lemons, juiced separately
Flaky salt, to taste
1 cup sprouted lentils, uncooked*
1 cup jasmine rice
⅓ cup plus 2 teaspoons extra-virgin olive oil, divided, plus
    more for the rice
1 pint cherry tomatoes (preferably Sun Golds, or the sweetest
    tomatoes you can find)
2 teaspoons Aleppo chili flakes (or red pepper flakes)
Cracked black pepper, to taste
2 tablespoons nutritional yeast
4 cups arugula

*If you can't find sprouted lentils, a can of brown lentils will do. Just rinse well, and warm with a bit of olive oil and salt.

Sliver (or mince—I personally love thin slices) your garlic. Add it to the juice from one large lemon with a good pinch of flaky salt. Set aside.

For lentils: Bring 3 cups of water to boil in a medium saucepan. Stir in lentils and let simmer for 6 minutes. Remove from heat and cover for an additional 2 minutes. Drain and return to the pan. Season with salt and add your lemon and garlic mixture. Taste and adjust salt to your personal liking. Not lemony enough? Go for it! Add more juice or even some zest.

For rice: Combine rice, a good glug of olive oil, and a sprinkle of salt with 1½ cups of water. Bring to a boil, stir, then reduce to a simmer and cover. It generally takes rice 10 to 15 minutes to fully cook, so sneak a peek occasionally to ensure it isn't sticking to the bottom of the pan. You want it nice and fluffy!

For tomatoes: Rinse and de-stem your little balls of goodness (yes, I'm talking about the tomatoes), and toss them into a medium-size sauté pan over medium-high heat with ⅓ cup olive oil and Aleppo pepper. Sprinkle generously with salt and pepper. Sauté for about 10 minutes or until the tomatoes start to burst (or collapse with a gentle smush of your wooden spoon. This is wildly satisfying).

For arugula: Mix juice of half a lemon with 2 teaspoons of extra-virgin olive oil, salt, and nutritional yeast. Toss the arugula in the dressing and hit with fresh black pepper.

The Joyous Moment: Combine lentils, rice, and tomatoes (make sure you get all that amazing, juicy tomato oil)! I personally like to let this combination cool for 5 to 10 minutes before I fold in the arugula because I despise wilted arugula. If you're Team Wilted, go wild. You also have the option to serve the arugula on the side as a salad, but, trust me—wait just a bit and toss it all together. Pure heaven. Bright, sweet, salty, peppery, creamy—folks, it has it all!

ON
RUNNING-AWAY FOOD

 Daniel Lavery

T HE MOST SUBSTANTIAL AND IMMEDIATE RESULT OF reading novels as a child was the shoring up of a dim-yet-tenacious conviction that somewhere out in the world was *good food*, good food of a type and quality and quantity that was either being consciously denied me in the present by certain unknown insurgent agents or whose preparation and provenance had long ago been forgotten. The best literary foods always appeared in the process of *running away*, that ceaseless and shared imaginative project of childhood everywhere.

My family lived in the northwest suburbs of Chicago, roughly equidistant between a Piggly Wiggly and a Jewel-Osco supermarket, which supplied my parents with sufficient material to feed us regularly and, I have no doubt, with the best of intentions. This meant skinless chicken breasts, sometimes with and sometimes without a sheet of Coca-Cola-colored teriyaki sauce blurted over them; Hamburger Helper (usually the beef stroganoff variety, but, on at least one memorable occasion, the cheeseburger macaroni made an appearance); massive and perpetually out-of-season raspberries in plastic clamshells; glasses of blue-tinged skim milk; foil-skinned triangles of Laughing Cow cheese; steamed broccoli; jealously guarded green boxes of SnackWell's diet devil's food cookie cakes and Healthy Choice diet ice cream; Trix pink-and-purple-swirl flavored yogurt; a newspaper-clipping recipe for coffee cake; Jif peanut butter (smooth, always; the primary texture of my childhood was *smoothness*); Little Caesars pizza on Friday nights; Oroweat whole-grain bread; a tusk-colored tub of Country Crock margarine; Eggo mini waffles on Sundays, two flats apiece, each flat containing four mini waffles, for a total of eight mini waffles per person, with Log Cabin maple-flavored syrup, microwaved for fifteen seconds before pouring.

But the type of book I liked best as a middle-grade, middle-class, middle-risk child always managed to combine the independence of running away with the conveniences of a secure household: Lucy Pevensie bolts out of England through the wardrobe and straight into afternoon tea; the Kincaid siblings tuck themselves into the Metropolitan Museum of Art and subsequently tuck into pie and coffee from the Automat (a true flower of the Midwest, I was overwhelmed by the glamour of the very idea of *automated coffee*); Liza and Annie of *Annie on My Mind* sharing baked beans and cheese sandwiches at the selfsame museum a decade or so later; Jesse's terrifyingly extravagant three-dollar lunch in *Bridge to Terabithia*; even Ramona Quimby's "tongue surprise" had an otherworldly appeal, as the only tongue I'd ever chewed had been my own, to say nothing of her basement feast of apples; the hoarded blueberries and river-cold bottles of milk available to the

Boxcar Children, whose tenure in the boxcar was disappointingly brief; Heidi's endless supply of toasted-cheese sandwiches; the dizzying array of savory pies available to Bilbo Baggins and the mice priests of *Redwall*, which often melded together into a single feast in my imagination.

Unlike my own ziplocked lunches, the sandwiches in these stories always seemed to arrive wrapped carefully in either waxed or buttered paper, often with a single ingredient: cheese sandwich, egg sandwich, ham sandwich. Cakes wrapped in napkins, stored in pockets that by necessity must have been bigger and more capacious than any pocket I'd ever worn in my life. Bread and cheese featured heavily in these fantasies, mostly because I didn't really know how to work the stove by myself yet, unlike *A Wrinkle in Time*'s maddeningly precocious Charles Wallace, whose ability to make hot cocoa at age five liquefied me with envy. The dream of running away to a world of greater freedom and *even greater convenience*! I knew I was destined for a life of Automat baked beans, of thick squares of pie, of cheese-only sandwiches, of loaves of bread not yet sliced, of buttered wedges of bannock cake, of a thermos of coffee with Cremora, whatever Cremora was—food that came only in the form of *wedges* and *squares* and *fat slices*, bound up in napkins and blotting paper and string, good *corner* food, food with an edge and a base and a foundation, food designed to hold its own structure right until coming to rest in the happy basement of the stomach. To be responsible for one's own coziness was the most ambitious promise of these books, to store up one's larder with future treasures, to catalog and memorize the scale and remit of all future meals in a fat lump wholly unrecognizable to the carefully apportioned, managed, and throttled allowance of pleasure of a SnackWell's cookie.

Then there was the food the television promised, mostly through reruns of old *Merrie Melodies* and *Little Lulu* cartoons, Dickensian plenty filtered through Errol Flynn's *The Adventures of Robin Hood*, what I thought of at the time as "king food" and later came to think of as "Renaissance Faire food"—a big hot onion at the end of a jeweled dagger, a brace of partridges, little hot pancakes tossed in the air and then down the throat in exaggerated gulps, roasted apples with skins too hot to handle by hand, the sort of food one claps at servants for more, with candles guttering in the background, bread ripped open and steaming, goblets of red and purple, big spiced halves of beast, chestnuts and sweetmeats, geese and gooseberries, a table riddled with plenty, set for both the wild man and the king, crying welcome.

The closest I came to such a table in real life was a fourth-grade field trip to Medieval Times, where we were encouraged to eat a tin plate's worth of rotisserie chicken with our hands, an experience so pleasurable to my eight-year-old appetite, I nearly blacked out before the joust. Boston Market's rotisserie chicken, until that moment the height of my culinary experience, would forever pale in comparison. I knew then, and tucked the knowledge safely away, that there was glory and satisfaction to be wrung from the world, if only for those willing to leave home in order to find and eat it. There were a thousand SnackWell's cookies to be chewed through first, but I had strong teeth from all that skim milk and could already see my way through to the other side.

THE RAT BIRTHDAY PIE

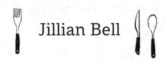

Jillian Bell

WHEN I WAS TWENTY-THREE, I RAN AWAY. OKAY, THAT'S incredibly dramatic. I went to London by myself for three weeks. Everyone in my family knew where I was. I just wanted to hook you in as a reader.

The trip had many traditional tourist highlights—I did cheesy tours, visited a small library on a boat, spent hours pretending I understood art in a museum, and had an unplanned photo shoot where I got headshots I still use to this day. I should *really* get updated headshots. . . . Back to the story! By the time my last night rolled around, I realized the one thing I had not yet done was the thing everyone claimed was a "must" while in London—eat a slice of banoffee pie, a traditional English dessert made with bananas, toffee, and cream. I could not return to the States* without having done this!

---

*The States: a reference to the United States made by London locals and American women trying too hard.

I threw on my peacoat, wool hat, and oversize scarf and hit the streets of Marylebone (the area I was in) to find that pie. I still don't know how to pronounce Marylebone to this day. Mar-lay-bone? Meryl(Streep)-lee-bone? Back to the story! I passed restaurant after restaurant, but no one had my precious dessert. It was getting late, and I was close to giving up . . . the baby. Okay, no baby. Just hooking you in again. Sorry. I was close to giving up my search when I stopped in a small shop near my flat.* The shop was the British equivalent to a 7-Eleven, and I needed a couple of things† for my trip home. On my way to the register, I passed a frozen-food section, and there it was . . . a frozen-as-shit banoffee pie. "Frozen . . . the way it's meant to be enjoyed," she said to herself.

I paid for my "hard as a rock" pie and skipped back to my place in Marylebone. (Mary-J-Blige?)

I packed my bags while doing several check-ins on the pie as it defrosted. There was a lot of finger-tapping the center of the pie followed by a woman saying out loud to no one, "Not ready yet!" After a long shower, the pie was what I would call "still not ready but you-can-stick-a-fork-in-it-ish." I got in my pajamas, grabbed the pie, and got comfy in bed. Here we go. I cut into the pie and took my first bite.

I'll never forget it. I've never simultaneously wanted everyone I knew to be there with me to try it while also not wanting a single soul around so I could eat it like a disgusting bridge troll.

I was in heaven. But as I went in for my eighty-third bite, I realized I was no longer alone. An English mouse, who was apparently *also* staying in my Airbnb, was watching me scarf down my somewhat frozen pie. We locked eyes for seven seconds, and I think I may have said "Hi."

*Flat: same thing as "the States" but about an apartment.
†A couple of things: tampons.

And then he ran back to the hole he was living in. I have to say, I do enjoy a mouse. But when you're staying in a different country and you find a mouse in your bedroom right before you're going to sleep . . . all you can think of is said mouse crawling into your mouth while you're passed out. So I stayed up the whole night, quietly nibbling on the best pie I had ever tasted while having periodic staring contests with Mickey when he'd reemerge.

When I got back, I tried to re-create the delicious experience sans rat. I wanted to give my pie a twist, and because I'm not a culinary genius, I did what everyone does to make themselves feel fancy. I added chocolate. But I'm an adult (she tells herself), so it's dark chocolate. (Feel free to be impressed! No? Cool.)

After several failed attempts, I did it! My friend Selyna came over to partake and coined it "The Birthday Pie" because . . . well, she wanted it for her birthday every year. I added "Rat" to the title for obvious reasons. So it's become my thing, and by "my thing" I mean I've made it a handful of times. (To be honest, I've made it for some of my friends' birthdays but never for Selyna's.) I guess the point of this story is to say, mice make me scarf sweets and I'm a bad friend.

JILLIAN BELL

Rat Birthday Pie

INGREDIENTS

FOR THE CRUST:

> 14 graham crackers
> ¼ cup granulated sugar
> 10 tablespoons unsalted butter, melted

FOR THE DARK CHOCOLATE TOFFEE:

> One 13.4-ounce can dulce de leche
> Pinch of salt
> ½ cup dark chocolate morsels
> (*Or* 1 jar of Stonewall Kitchen dark chocolate sea salt caramel sauce if you're just like, "fuck it.")

FOR THE WHIPPED CREAM:

> 1 pint (2 cups) heavy whipping cream, cold
> ½ cup powdered sugar
> 1 teaspoon pure vanilla extract

OTHER ITEMS:

> 2 ripe bananas (or 3 if you love bananas)
> 1 regular-size (roughly 1.55-ounce) milk chocolate bar (Put in the fridge so it gets cold while you're baking.)

RECIPE

Grease a 9-inch tart pan or pie dish.

If you have a food processor, add the graham crackers and sugar, and pulse until they look like bread crumbs. Then drizzle in the melted butter while the food processor is still running. (If you don't have a food processor, throw your graham crackers into a ziplock bag and pound the shit out of them—it's exercise and therapy. Then mix with the sugar and melted butter in a bowl.)

Pour the mixture into the prepared tart pan or pie dish. Press the crumbs firmly into the dish and up the sides. Refrigerate for 1 hour.

When the hour is up, it's time to make the chocolate toffee. Place the dulce de leche in a heatproof bowl over a pot of simmering water. Add salt and that (fancy adult) dark chocolate slowly. Stir until the chocolate and dulce de leche are blended.

(If you went the "fuck it" route, take the jar of dark chocolate sea salt caramel sauce and scoop all the remnants into a small saucepan. Let it simmer for a few minutes and stir often. Don't let it boil. Just heat it enough to get it warm.)

Take the crust out of the fridge and make sure it's solid. Then pour the warm toffee on top of the crust. This is the delicious bottom layer. Refrigerate for 30 minutes, until cooled and set.

When the toffee is set, slice the bananas and spread them on top of the toffee in two layers (or three if you're *wild*).

Put the heavy whipping cream, powdered sugar, and vanilla extract in the bowl of a stand mixer or a medium to large mixing bowl. Beat these ingredients together, starting on low speed and increasing to high speed as it begins to firm up. Beat until stiff peaks form. Spread this as the final layer on top of the bananas.

Take the milk chocolate bar out of the fridge. Use a cheese grater to shave the chocolate over the top. Happy birthday, ya rat.

LE PAN BAGNAT DE PAPA

 Garance Doré

I GREW UP ON THE CORSICAN COAST. MY PARENTS, IRÈNE AND Louis, had a restaurant there, the exact restaurant you're imagining. An open terrace overlooking the turquoise sea. Beautiful people at the bar and sumptuous freshly caught fish on the plates.

My father was the chef, always hardworking in his kitchen, and my mother was the flamboyant front-of-house figure. My brother, my sister, and I didn't see them much during the summer. They were working day and night.

During that time, like all the kids in our village, we became little wildlings, little princes and princesses of our island, free as life itself, protected by the nature all around us.

Morning started with the smells of coffee and cigarettes—remember, it was the eighties—mixed with those of bread, butter, and jam. After breakfast we were free for the whole day. In the evenings, I'd try to catch octopus at the beach down below. But when I heard my mother call "A taaaaaaaable!!!" it was my sign the day was over.

Eating in the middle of the day was more complicated. We didn't really have a private kitchen. If we were hungry, we'd have to catch the staff's meal, which happened every day at 11:30 a.m., right before the midday service. If I made it in time, I'd find myself sitting with the team of twelve or more—the sous chefs, the commis, the waiters, and the bartenders. There was a raucous camaraderie, a colorful *Kitchen Confidential* sense of humor that I loved. They knew the next few hours would be spent in the warm hell that is a summer restaurant's kitchen, and you could feel the adrenaline running through their veins. Throughout, my father sat at the head of the table, silent and focused.

Oh, I loved the 11:30 meal. But some days, I forgot the time and I missed it.

When that happened, unless I found a seat at one of my friends' tables, the only thing left for me to do was to get right in the middle of the restaurant's bustling kitchen and ask my dad for something to eat. But he was busy and didn't want me foraging around. And if you've ever known a chef, you know *busy* for them means "on the brink of madness, pretty much crazy, might explode," which made the whole endeavor slightly scary.

I remember one day in particular. I had just made my rare kitchen appearance, scavenging for something to eat, but was greeted with "Not again!!!" Based on the disgruntled expression on his face, I thought, *Whoops, this might be the last time.* I'd never seen him so frustrated.

I considered escaping but waited outside, ready to get scolded.

But when he came out, I was surprised by the gentle expression I saw on his face. He offered me a little bag.

"Here is your pique-nique, mon enfant. I made you a pan bagnat. Do you know pan bagnat? It's the best sandwich in the entire world."

I kissed him thank-you and left the way I had come, running and jumping and falling, with my little bag in my hand. I sat down under a tree to eat my pan bagnat. I still remember the juiciness, the deliciousness, and all the love. The five minutes he had taken out of his busy moment for his mischievous child. And I remember thinking, *Papa is right. This is the best sandwich in the entire world.*

LE PAN BAGNAT DE PAPA

MY SANDWICH

 Kavi Ahuja Moltz

I HUDDLED OVER MY LUNCH, SHIELDING IT AS BEST AS I COULD from the view of my classmates, holding my breath.

Someone had caught a glimpse or a whiff. I was already rattled by the rowdy morning school bus, which had become a social mine-field, and it turned out the cafeteria was no different. They were onto me and my sandwich. I felt defeated. I pushed aside feelings of shame at my offending lunch and took another bite. Despite the whispers, I enjoyed my meal. The tangy layer of spicy green chutney suspended between two slices of white Wonder bread brought me back to the comforts of the home I had left that morning. The home I had left to come to battle on school grounds. Well, it was just Catholic school, where I spent my days being intimidated by blonder, paler, and less hairy girls. Being young hurts.

Around me, my chatty classmates confidently ate their ham sand-wiches and drank their skim milk. One had the name "Summer." I couldn't understand her luck, to be comfortably floating through life with that skin and that hair, and to be named after something so commonplace as a season—literally named after sunshine. And then there was mine, which I finally gave up and shortened to avoid further butchering. Kavita became Kuh-vee-duh, pronounced with a *d* where there was no *d*. Summer never had to repeat or spell out her name. Summer never had to take a pair of scissors to her leg hair simply because her mother wouldn't let her shave. She had blond hair, and to me, the way it glistened was prettier than bare legs anyway.

Back to the cafeteria. Their aversion to the smell and sight of my lovingly packed Indian lunches was discouraging for a few hours. Little did they know the chutney sandwich and the foil-wrapped mini samosas were just the tip of the iceberg. A mere gateway drug to the strange and pungent items lurking in the cupboards of my house. Were my classmates to come over, what might they find? What might they smell? I'm not sure I ever invited them to find out. During the school day, I felt self-conscious about my food, my religion, my skin, my body. But every day when I walked back into my house, I was welcomed by the warm waft of blooming cardamom and toasted coriander seeds. It was comfort, and I could feel free at home.

Growing up, my parents' goal for my brother and me was assimilation—that we would never be perceived as people for whom English was a second language, that we would grow up feeling like we belonged in their adopted country. But at home, India ruled in all other ways: blaring bhajans, chanting prayers, spicy breakfasts, forced Bharatanatyam dance classes. The meals were all from my mother's kitchen, via her mother's kitchen, and so on down the years. It was the world I knew, and one that embraced me.

That comfort was not only in the food but also in the gathering. I have so much love for hosting just because of growing up with so much of it. I often wonder how my parents did it all. I recall hundreds of casually put together joyful evenings. An abundance of dishes crowded the worn lace tablecloth, kids weaved between adult limbs and passed out on sofas. Babysitters were not even a concept we had heard of. Instead we perused plates of candy-colored wafers, deep-fried and puffy. Seas of spiced nuts, artful platters of crunchy chaat, and dishes of various namkeens (out of which stuck the ubiquitous communal teaspoon) invited guests to scoop bits into their cupped palms. I still crave the chili cheese toasts made with tinned Amul cheese, finely chopped red onion, and tiny green chilis. After each gathering, my parents stayed up cleaning until two a.m., then woke in the morning before most of the world, and were off to work again on a Saturday. The warmth and nostalgia of the evening sustained them, helping to brace against the scattered discriminations they would encounter the next day. I could tell they also experienced the same contrast of home and the outside world.

We never really spoke about it, but for us kids there was a camaraderie among my Indian friends from that time. Though we were ignored at school, we had one another. We had shared language, food, weird names, and strict parents. Later, in my college years, some friends told me they were envious that I belonged to a culture. That I fit in someplace just because of who I was. My school friends told me that, and I just thought, *Oh, the irony.*

Now when I have a dinner party, I pull out my mom's recipes when I want to impress. I love to invite our American friends into our home and greet them with the fragrances of my childhood Indian kitchen. To celebrate the dishes I've loved all my life and no longer feel self-conscious about. If I have time, I'll make fresh green chutney to go with some delicious little fried item—so simple to put together (yet labor intensive, as you need to pick the coriander leaves from the stems). My mother did this for my school sandwiches, and I still perceive it as an act of love. The chutney captures everything I love about our food—bright, bold, and spicy. It's the same green goop that my classmates made me self-conscious about, but nowadays my guests just kind of drink it up.

THE BEARDED LADY TRUCKSTOP AND COFFEE SHOP

 Silas Howard

HE FIRST TIME I BURNED THE VEGETARIAN CHILI AT THE
Bearded Lady Truckstop and Coffee Shop (under the sign that
read A PLACE FOR DYKES, QUEERS, FREAKS, AND OTHER PEOPLE), a café
my best pals and I owned in our early twenties in San Francisco, it
was a crisis. Out of necessity, meaning we had no more ingredients
to make another pot or money to buy more ingredients, we had to
make do. (The adage "My bad luck was in fact my good luck" comes to
mind for most of the things I learned by starting that café in the early
nineties.)

The burned chili turned out to simply need a new perspective and
a new name. Hartman, a genderqueer pal with a dark maroon mohawk
à la Travis Bickle from *Taxi Driver*, could actually cook and elevated our

menu when they joined me and my best friend, Harry Dodge, shortly after we opened our doors. Hartman stopped me just before I scraped the burned bottom of the chili pot. Like an EMT in an emergency, he got to work slicing tofu, adding honey and spices, and making a new sign that transformed "burned vegetarian chili" into "smoked BBQ chili."

And thus a new special at the Bearded Lady was born.

Harry and I, both queer in-betweeners looking for a community and dreaming of becoming artists, couldn't stand working for other people. We decided to try our own thing by saving up money we'd stolen and some cash I'd gotten from a settlement for a motorcycle accident. We didn't understand the economics of owning a small business or really even how to run a café, but we wanted to create a place where our friends could gather and the artists around us could put on shows.

The Bearded Lady, long and narrow like a lane at the smallest bowling alley, was the queer home we desperately needed. It became a place for many friends getting clean and an equal number of friends losing their minds.

The first week we opened, we had no money to buy pastries, so we ordered samples from different local bakeries and sold those. We pirated our electricity (which meant the hot plate and coffeemaker couldn't run simultaneously or the fuse would blow), scrambled our eggs with the espresso machine's steamer, and made soups on a hot plate we had to hide from the health inspector because apparently you need seven sinks to make soup and we had only six.

We had queer Seders at the café, and on New Year's my bandmate Leslie Mah made egg rolls from a recipe taught to her by her family. Another made homemade tamales from her grandmother's recipe.

We reimagined the family table—hell, we rebuilt it—out of old metal scraps, disc brakes, and rebar from the junkyard welded together.

The café, a performance in and of itself, was also a gallery and performance space. The first officially commissioned work featured a student from the San Francisco Art Institute who opened fifty-two cans of tuna fish, one for each state and territory, dumped the tuna on the floor, and stomped on the growing pile. The cement floor held the scent of fish for weeks, attracting all the neighborhood cats.

The café attracted all kinds of strays. Visiting queers from all over and occasional luminaries like Joan Jett, Vivian Bond, Kathy Acker, and Catherine Opie spent time at the Bearded Lady, and all ate that chili in one form or another for almost a decade, along with our neighborhood regulars.

Our storefront used to be a small Latino church. The apartments upstairs housed a lot of drug addicts and people just a step away from SROs. The FOR RENT sign on our café had been up for over a year before we moved in. Juanita lived upstairs; she had stringy black hair, a missing front tooth, a four-year-old kid, and an abusive ex-boyfriend. Her head hung low, eyes peeking up as she talked. She laughed nervously all the time. Little bursts of forced breath, not joyful so much as a laugh begging for permission to stay. Juanita came down to the café one day with a sketch pad and asked us to look at her artwork. The pages were filled with wispy pencil drawings of women in various S&M scenes— female Tom of Finland kind of stuff. She got clean and sober, got rid of the abusive ex, and continued to fill her book with drawings. And we put up her first art show.

Calamity Joe was another regular. She was a wild, quick-witted, butch dyke—part Monty Python, part punk James Dean—a sexy little sadomasochist mystery who belonged to a queer gang called the HAGS SF. Their motto: "United we tag, divided we run." She was a voracious reader of feminist theory, intensely sharp, and always on the wrong side of popular opinion—that is to say, she was ahead of her time. Of course she had a favorite goddess: Freyja, a Viking who rides a chariot pulled by two cats. She wrote the opening lyrics to Tribe 8's, my band's, first ever song, spoofing the political correctness and gentleness of mainstream lesbian culture. The song would later fuel a protest when we played it at the Michigan Womyn's Music Festival, which was covered by everything from *Ms.* magazine to *Billboard*, but that is another story.

When Joe was off her medication, she used to sit by the window talking loudly to herself and rocking back and forth. One day I approached Joe slowly and said, "You can stay here, Joe, but you've got to keep it down a bit." Looking at me with a sparky, self-righteous concentration, Joe said, "I'm. Working. On. A. Performance. Piece."

Back then in San Francisco you never lost your mind, you were simply working on a performance piece.

Near the end, Calamity Joe was home—and family-less, blind without her glasses, and sleeping on the sidewalks of the Tenderloin, occasionally scoring a spot on the heating grates known as the "Tenderloin Hot Springs." She was an artist without a proper stage—pure hope against the odds—and we were all her audience, held by her quicksilver brain and irreverence. Calamity Joe died of complications from hepatitis C and cancer after decades of battling addiction. Drugs had become a solution for a disenfranchised group. For some, creating a home is a dangerous act.

Miss Kitty Litter Green was a legendary drag queen and painter who gave no fucks and toured Japan with her band, Clipped Out Recipes. She acted in quite a few campy Japanese films and even in shows like *Buffy the Vampire Slayer*. By the time I met her, she was in the early stages of dementia from AIDS-related complications. Her two caretakers brought her to our café every Saturday morning. She was still, to a T, a perfect lady, moving slowly, stopping time as a line formed out the door and she lost herself in the world of ordering breakfast. Each decision was made, then remade, as we waited and wrote stuff down and rewrote it. It was her finest hour and she made every minute count; she would not be rushed. So we waited, eyes on the line of customers behind her, and hoped that one particular sentence would come out, the only thing she ever ended up ordering: "Pesto eggs and . . . toast, no butter." Ahh, at last, we raced to the food-prep area and stuck the order up, arms raised like a pugilist's, while Miss Kitty walked, slower than anything in that room, to one of the metal tables of the café.

Miss Kitty simultaneously broke our hearts and frustrated us—we were too young to process all the loss. We had places to be, and appointments to keep, and no time for a slow fading star.

The unsinkable Bambi Lake, part Marlene Dietrich, part Courtney Love—in a slip dress, fur coat, and jewelry—was often found high on speed and holding me hostage behind the counter. She'd been 86'd out of most clubs and restaurants by then, but before addiction, mental health issues, and houselessness got ahold of her, Bambi was a legendary chanteuse and performed alongside legends like Sylvester and Divine, Henry Rollins, The Stranglers, and Exene Cervenka from the band X.

She was an anomaly not only for her art (her song "The Golden Age of Hustlers" is performed all over the world) but her age; very few

in our community had lived to fifty due to AIDS, and even fewer trans women survived. She told fantastical tales of touring with Bowie and hanging with Billy Idol. The stories were too well told for anyone to care if they were true or not; you just had to believe. One of the most notorious ones was the "Bombi" story, in which she was arrested for calling in an explosive threat to a Rolling Stones after-party in the late nineties after being denied admission.

Another raconteur regular, Kris Kovick, a queer butch, twenty years older than we were, lovingly referred to as Uncle Kris, taught us the most important tool of survival—a wicked sense of humor, especially around one's self. After being diagnosed with terminal cancer, she would come to the café, a small grill tucked under her arm and a bag of meat in the other. Somewhere she had heard that cooked meat helped fight cancer, so Sunday's menus were either grilled chicken or "pork on a fork," freely given away to customers. Kovick not only mentored us in life but also in her dying. She had a list of top-ten things she loved about cancer, number one being that no one asked you to help them move anymore. She also paid our rent when needed, telling us how important our art was. Everyone knew that if you needed a place to stay, an ear to listen, or a moment of rest, you could go to her house and she'd make you a sandwich. They are still the best damn sandwiches I've ever had.

I interviewed Kovick before she died for a short documentary, *What I Love About Dying*, about the shows she curated at the Bearded Lady from 1991 to 1993. One in particular, titled *Together Forever*, featured a pair of twins conjoined at the head whom she booked to perform. "Just remarkable performers," she said, but there was a caveat: she wasn't sure that they would really show up. "They were always fighting," she said, "because one of them was a folk singer, and the other one hated folk music."

Next door to the Bearded Lady, a postage-size avant-garde gallery called Kiki opened shortly after we did. Despite a short existence, or perhaps because of it, Kiki is the stuff of legend. Rick Jacobsen, a cultural impresario and artist, turned his AIDS diagnosis into a second chance at life and opened the tiny space. Kiki hosted over 150 artists and performers in its eighteen months of existence, among them future international artists: Lutz Bacher, Nao Bustamante, Jerome Caja, Frances Stark, Chris Johanson, Nayland Blake, Catherine Opie, Rex Ray, and Kevin Killian.

His first exhibition, *Caca at Kiki*, featured wickedly humorous works dealing with scatology, which many had to contend with during the pandemic. Sick humor and art kept us sane as "outsiders of the outsiders." On a weekend evening, you could purchase a veggie dog and a coffee in the Bearded Lady, walk about fifteen paces down a narrow corridor and through a back room, exit onto the patio, and take a left into the back room of Kiki. Rick became family too. If I had bought one piece from each show I'd be sitting on a fortune.

Kiki's last show, a tribute to Yoko Ono, was titled *This Is Not Her*. Evidence that the gallery had made the scene came in the form of a phone message from Ono herself, who called to say, "This is her. Yoko! The proof is in the pudding." Then she let out one of her famous, chilling shrieks.

Kiki closed after Jacobsen grew too weak to sustain the spectacle and returned to his mother's home in Wisconsin for his final year, promising to reincarnate as Michael Jackson's first child.

Two decades after the Bearded Lady closed, those of us who remain are still in touch. We have the world's most annoyingly long group text, where we share wild stories from the early days and pictures of our kids, who are looking to likely be as weird as we were.

That chili recipe, the regular and the BBQ version, is now our family recipe, passed down along with so many stories of people who were and who could have been. Each of us has their own version, their own substitute, their own magic ingredient, but it took all of us to make it the special thing it was.

POULET YASSA

 Gabourey Sidibe

I AM NOT A GOOD COOK. I WANT TO BLAME MY INABILITY TO cook on something. Maybe it's because I'm a millennial. Maybe it's because I'm too busy with all of my work. Maybe it's because I was raised by a single mom who was usually too tired to come home from work and cook, so we ate a lot of takeout. Maybe it's because I myself am a very busy mom of two cats, and there's just no time to take over the world all day *and* successfully cook a pot of rice! Honestly, I use every single one of these excuses and more to explain my inability to cook and feed myself, but when the pandemic hit, all of these excuses became null and void.

Suddenly, there was nothing but time. Nowhere to go, nowhere to be except for home. Takeout was available at a minimum, but everything from the outside world felt too dangerous to bring into our homes. It was best to make our own food after braving the grocery store and fighting with strangers over packs of toilet tissue and the last pack of frozen turkey legs. Oh my God! Do you remember early in the pandemic? Using Clorox wipes to wipe down everything you brought into the house? Spraying Lysol on every piece of mail in your mailbox? I personally would come home from the store, strip at the door, and immediately throw whatever I was wearing into the dryer in order to kill any COVID germs that might've smuggled their way into my home via the gloves I wore to touch everything. We were so young and dumb in the beginning of the pandemic, weren't we?

Around the second month of the pandemic, I realized that there was finally time to learn all of the things that I had convinced myself there was no time to learn. Like yoga! Or knitting! Or cooking! I decided that I would try to re-create my favorite food from childhood that my dad made: Poulet Yassa.

Poulet Yassa is basically marinated chicken over that pot of rice I may never be able to cook correctly. The chicken is marinated in lemon juice or lime juice, along with onions, garlic, ginger, Dijon mustard, and Scotch bonnet pepper, for at least eight hours or overnight. While created in Senegal, Yassa has become popular in the whole of West Africa. It's delicious, with simple ingredients, and is almost impossible to mess up, so it felt like the perfect place to start! Not only is Yassa pretty simple to make but it calls back really vivid memories of my childhood. Yassa has always kind of felt like an extended family member to me.

I am Senegalese. Well, half Senegalese on my dad's side. I like to pretend I'm fully Senegalese when America is being especially heinous, and, as I am a black woman, that's most days. Senegal is a country in West Africa where my dad was born and where he still calls home several months of the year. I actually haven't been since I was a very small child. My dad lives in Brooklyn, New York, but it feels like every time I turn around, he's either just coming back from Senegal or on his way there. He still has a lot of family there. And not just brothers, sisters, nieces, and nephews, but several other children in Senegal. I believe they are all grown up and in their twenties now. Maybe older . . . or younger, for that matter. I don't know anything about them. I don't know what they look like or even what their names are. I've never asked, and my dad has, as far as I can tell, never thought to share anything about them with me.

Senegal is a Muslim country, and as a little girl, I was expected to grow into a proper Muslim woman. This meant learning to cook, clean, and take care of babies, among other things. Most of these lessons were taught to me by my dad. He would put a chair in the kitchen and have me stand on it so that I could watch and help him to peel and cut onions. He would instruct me to pull all of the skin off the chicken, and he'd inspect my work when I was done. He'd cut the lemons in half and have me squeeze every bit of juice out of them with my bare hands, and then teach me to use a spoon when my little hands weren't strong enough. Because of my young age and my whining, he'd let me skip the very hot Scotch bonnet pepper altogether. To this day, every time I eat African food prepared by anyone else, I'm always surprised by how spicy it usually is, but back then, Dad and I would make the mildest possible version of Poulet Yassa for our small family of four. This was, of course, before all of his other families came around. We were his first family, but back then we had no idea that we would never be his only family.

Deciding to learn to make authentic Senegalese food during the pandemic was an easy decision. There was time to marinate things correctly, and, thanks to the internet, a million and one recipes to try. I even had a willing participant to taste everything for me: my boyfriend,

Brandon. He used to just be my boyfriend, but the pandemic quickly upgraded him to a live-in boyfriend. At that point in our relationship, he was pretty sure I could do no wrong and thought I hung the moon. And he was more than excited to eat anything I put in front of him. Even undercooked Cornish hens I thought I could make in an air fryer! That was a hard lesson for both of us.

So one day in between COVID naps and binge-watching *90 Day Fiancé*, I jumped on my laptop to look for Yassa recipes. They all said something a little different from each other, but I tried my best to follow along with what felt right. I didn't think to call the only expert I knew.

Dad and I don't talk much. I am not his favorite child, and he is not my favorite parent. We can go months without talking to each other, and when we do, it's usually through obligation, and more often than not involves a monetary transaction on my part. We can both be quite judgmental of each other. There's a chasm with a river of pain between us, a river, if I'm being honest, that flows in both directions.

Google gave me a list of what I needed and instructions on how to prepare it all, and I got to work, documenting every step of the process by taking pictures with my phone. I planned to send every picture to Dad to make sure everything looked the way it was supposed to but decided not to. When it was completely done and the full meal had been plated, including my first successful pot of rice, I sent him the photo of the finished product along with a text saying "I finally learned to make Yassa."

"Save me some," he responded.

"It's really good too! I used two lemons and a lime," I said.

"Looks good," he replied.

And that was it. Dad and I *really* don't talk much.

Brandon enjoyed the food. He cleaned his plate. Again, he thinks I'm close to perfect, so that's expected. But Dad said, "Looks good." *That* meant something.

The strange thing about absent fathers is how little they give you and how massive that little always feels. It's like your heart and your mind can't agree on what's valuable and what's garbage.

As the pandemic dragged on from winter to spring, through summer, and to fall, Brandon, my live-in boyfriend, upgraded his position again, eventually becoming my fiancé. This was a surprise to no one (especially not to me because I accidentally found my engagement ring months before he actually popped the question), as we were in one of those relationships where you can clearly see and hear the wedding bells chiming in the distance every time we looked at each other.

Pretty early in the relationship, way before the pandemic, Brandon wanted to meet my parents. Both of them. He has divorced parents and was excited for me to meet his family, and he made it clear that he wanted to meet the people who spawned me. Brandon is a very family-oriented person who talks to his parents and his brother pretty often. Every week, if not every day. I, on the other hand, am . . . kind of just out here living. I don't even know all of my siblings' names! But Brandon wanted to meet my family, so fine!

We ended up going to New York City, where my family is, and spent two days having meals with them. Night one, we met Dad at a Senegalese fusion restaurant I found in Harlem. It was just the three of us, and Brandon asked Dad for embarrassing stories about me as a child. Dad shared the time when we were in a cab during a snowstorm, and I thought it was a great idea to open the door of the car while it was moving, resulting in everyone freaking out and me getting a spanking

once we got home. Though I was maybe five years old at the time, I remember it clearly, and I stand by that great idea! My theory was that the car would stop if the door was opened, and I had to test that theory. I did it for science! I did it for humanity! I shouldn't have been punished. I should've been awarded the National Medal of Science!

Then Dad told us about how Muslim people used to be Jewish people. This was surprising. Not just because I couldn't fathom how two different religions that are far away from each other geographically and have followers that look so different from each other were once one, but also because this was somehow my father showing his approval of my boyfriend. Brandon's Jewish. I hadn't considered Dad's approval because it wasn't something I wanted or needed. What was most surprising was that I liked having it. Brandon absolutely relished this new information and felt that it was a sign that my dad really liked him. Spoiler alert: Things have changed.

Dad ordered extra food to take home to his family, and Brandon and I split the bill. Sometime after dinner, Brandon told me that he was pretty traditional, and so when the time came, he would ask my dad for my hand in marriage. Gross.

Before Brandon, I had been single my entire adult life. I am quite grown up and independent. My whole body, my hands included, belong to me and me alone. There's no man in the world whose *yes* or *no* can either keep or give me or any part of me away. My independence has been hard-won and I'm far from giving it up to any man—whether it's the father who sired me or the man who wants to marry me. As far as I was concerned, Dad didn't own me and Brandon marrying me didn't mean that he now got to own me.

I have a tendency to be quite literal in my thinking, and though I know that the transfer of my hand from my father to my spouse is an archaic tradition and symbolic, it still didn't sit right with me. It's caveman shit. I told Brandon not to bother and that my relationship with my dad wasn't appropriate for that sort of thing but that I ultimately didn't care. But he wanted to do it anyway.

That was before he realized just how absent my dad truly is.

For my first pandemic birthday, Brandon got all of my close friends and family members to make me a short video message sending love and birthday wishes.

My dad was not included. Brandon tried really hard to include him, but Dad never answered him when he reached out to him on Facebook. At some point I called Dad to check up on him. The call went to voice mail, so I left a message. My dad didn't respond for over three months. At least twice a week Brandon asked if I had talked to my dad yet, and every time I answered no, he became more shocked and sadder for me.

I wasn't sad at all. I was still learning to perfect my cooking.

Each time I prepared it, I wouldn't serve it if it didn't taste like Dad's. I got so good at making Yassa that I made it for friends for their birthdays! I made it for small COVID-safe gatherings we had at home. Soon I moved on to other Senegalese dishes like maffe (peanut butter stew), fataya (meat pie), and plantains. While I never grew to be the proper Muslim woman Dad planned for me to be, I could fake it for a few hours in the kitchen.

Time passed, and eventually Brandon abandoned his traditional plans and just asked me to marry him, without my dad's blessing. I sent Dad a text with a picture of Brandon and me and my engagement ring. He responded by saying, "Marriage is based on love and trust, so I wish you the best happy union." Great! He didn't seem to care about the caveman shit of being asked for my hand in marriage! Or so I thought . . .

Brandon and I live in Los Angeles. His mom, stepdad, and brother live in Chicago, and his dad and stepmom are in Arizona. My family is all in New York City. When we all got vaccinated, we basically went on a tour to see the family we'd been so spread apart from. When we booked our flight to New York City, I thought it'd be a great idea to have Brandon taste Dad's Yassa. He *was* the master, after all, and I was so excited to not only have my dad's cooking again but also for Brandon to experience the better parts of my dad and not just those absent parts when he is hard to reach.

I planned everything! I asked Dad for a shopping list and went to get the groceries myself. We were going to have dinner at my mom's apartment, which she shares with my older brother, Ahmed. I went to straighten up the day before and made sure there was room for everyone and that there was space in the kitchen for Dad to prepare dinner in. I used to live in this apartment, and it would be the first time Brandon would see the home I grew up in and the first time he would be around my entire, small four-member family. I was very excited.

The night of the dinner, Dad showed up with two small children.

A ten-year-old boy I'd met only once before when he was five, and a five-year-old girl I had never met. Dad greeted me by rubbing my stomach and saying hello to my empty womb. Perhaps wishful thinking on his part, but I assured him I was not pregnant as he continued moving through the very small apartment. He saw Brandon, extended his hand to shake Brandon's, and very confidently said, "Donovan! Hello! How are you?"

"Brandon, Dad! His name is Brandon," I corrected, and then asked to be introduced to the children he had brought with him.

The girl, my sister, was named Asma, and the boy's name was Ahmed. If you're keeping count, *yes*, I have an older brother Ahmed and a ten-year-old brother, also named Ahmed. Why my dad needed two sons named Ahmed and born twenty-nine years apart, I'll never know. None of my business. Can you imagine a more awkward dinner party? Hold on to your butts!

Dad cooked in the kitchen in between long phone calls in French. He didn't try to converse with anyone else in the apartment. Meanwhile, big Ahmed and Brandon talked about music they listen to. Asma and I played games on Mom's iPad. Brandon showed Mom pictures of himself as a child, and she laughed as he told her funny stories of his childhood. I taught the kids how to play rock, paper, scissors. At some point Brandon and I were tickling the kids and watching YouTube with them. Dad didn't interact with anyone. Just the stove and his phone. This wasn't odd behavior from Dad. He's always been pretty quiet and a bit standoffish. No biggie.

When the food was finished, we all ate together without talking much at all. When the night was done, Brandon and I went back to our hotel, and Dad and his kids left soon after too. The next day I went back to Mom's apartment, and Ahmed told me that after Brandon and I left, Dad, who had barely spoken more than two words the entire night, said, "That guy Brandon is crazy. He's up under Gabourey like he's trying to protect his investment."

Absent fathers really are a trip. Dad doesn't know me. Dad doesn't know my value. Dad knows what I do for a living, and he knows how to dial my number when he needs money. Dad confuses my money with my value, and his scope of me is so narrow that he can't imagine how anyone else might see anything else of value in me.

Ahmed thought it was a joke. I didn't. I thought it was sad and il-luminating to know how my dad feels about me. Plenty of people see my mate, Brandon, and think he couldn't possibly actually love me. I am fat and black, and he is not, so that must mean he is in a relation-ship with me for any reason other than love. I've heard this theory before but always from complete strangers. None of my friends, or his friends and family, are surprised by our relationship. Brandon's parents tell me how much happier he is with me than they've ever known him to be. None of my family has suggested that Brandon is anything but completely and utterly in love with me. Except for my dad. Dad, who on several occasions had asked me to invest in some business he was trying to get off the ground, made a "joke" about Brandon trying to protect his investment in me, as if all I've ever been, and will ever be, is a cartoon bag of money with dollar signs across me.

Ahmed also told me that Dad was salty and upset that Brandon didn't ask him for my hand in marriage. That I just "got engaged out of nowhere." I found this to be baffling, as I am a thirty-eight-year-old woman, but for Brandon's sake, I called Dad to discuss his comment about my being an investment for Brandon. Dad denied it, but I assure you, he said it. He lied about having said it because it wasn't a joke and he knew it was hurtful. That's why he said it when Brandon and I weren't around to hear it.

I also told Dad that I knew he was mad and felt slighted because Brandon hadn't asked him for permission to marry me and that he could blame me for that. Not Brandon. I explained that we don't have the kind of daddy-daughter relationship that would make Brandon asking him for permission to marry me appropriate. He didn't disagree.

Absent fathers *know* that they are absent. Neither of us is in this relationship. Dad isn't showing up to father-daughter dances only to be stood up by me. We are both staying home.

I went on to say that him wanting to pass off my hand to Brandon in marriage is caveman shit that I don't subscribe to, and even if I did, he never responded to Brandon, so if he was holding on to any offense about that, it was time to let it go. The conversation ended.

Dad never admitted to what he said and therefore never apologized for it. I also didn't apologize for not considering *my daddy* when I was ready to marry a man at my big age. Just like every other conversation that seems to widen that chasm between us and trouble the river of hurt beneath us, this too ended without a resolution. Real life doesn't seem to have any real endings.

We take a lot from our parents. They usually raise us with the best of intentions, and they give us more love than they know they are capable of. My father's love for me is probably deeper than I can imagine. And my love for him is endless. Endless, not painless.

Much like a stove, I've learned what parts of my dad are safe to touch and what parts are hot enough to burn me. I'm sure he's learned those same rules about me. I take what parts of him I can use, and the parts that I can't I respectfully leave with him. He has more wives and children than I can count, and I'm more than sure that another daughter, who *is* his favorite, will insist that her future spouse ask Dad for permission to marry her.

Not me though. I'm just here for the chicken.

APRICOT CHICKEN

 iO Tillett Wright

THE PROBLEM CAME FROM AN APP CALLED DINNER SPIN-ner. You selected a protein, a serving size, and how long you wanted to pretend to know how to cook, then the spinner would make you a suggestion.

I was twenty-five, living in a Brooklyn shoebox with a "room-mate" who paid to sleep in my closet. I couldn't fit a dinner table in my apartment, but I yearned to feed my friends. We subsisted on deli sandwiches for every time of day—egg and cheese in the morning, sa-lami and mayo in the afternoons, and meatball subs after the bar. So I wanted to make something special, a home-cooked meal.

I chose chicken, for eight, ready in an hour, and spun the spinner. The horrifying confluence of elements it asked me to purchase, mix together, and serve for human consumption would haunt me for over a decade. They were:

3 packets powdered onion soup mix

2 cans apricots

1½ bottles Russian dressing

8 chicken breasts

All I had to do was mix everything but the chicken together in a bowl, pour the mixture over the meat, and cook it in the oven for 1 hour.

I'd never heard of Russian dressing or powdered soup mix, but I took my twenty dollars and left the house with an open heart.

I should have known something was wrong when my local Bushwick supermarket sent me to the dollar store to find the dressing. Ever optimistic, I thought, *Oh. Obscure. Chic.*

The small Korean woman at the dollar store cocked her head strangely when I asked for Russian dressing, then led me to a section high above the rest of the condiments. She gestured aloft at a beige metal shelf bending at the center. I peered into the crevice above her scalp, and there in the back, between twelve-year-old bottles of Newman's Own and something cubed, in Spanish and cloaked in dust, were the two bottles I needed for my feast. I took them, two boxes of couscous, and a ninety-nine-cent disposable turkey roasting tray, and trotted home, triumphant.

I like sweet and savory. I like sauce. I didn't know the difference between moist chicken and the mouthful of hay I served my friends; I thought I was killing it. I was a poor artist kid, high on benevolence. To be fair to my friends, they ate it, shoveling forkfuls and sputtering conversational kernels of couscous until the heat-snarled roasting pan was bare. I mistook their enthusiasm for enjoyment, not raw need, and felt quite pleased with myself. So much that for the next four years, I made a bimonthly tradition of chosen family dinner and made the same dish every time. The dollar store ordered more Russian dressing for me, I bought a real glass baking dish, and I deleted Dinner Spinner. It had retched forth everything I needed in the perfect dinner party dish—we were done.

A few years later, I moved to Los Angeles. Buckling under heartbreak, I taught myself to actually cook. Family dinners became elaborate experiments with recipes from real chefs, often taking hours to hit the table, often missing the mark. Apricot chicken was quickly forsaken for dishes that required specialty grocery stores, and I made a new crop of friends who had never experienced my signature masterpiece.

I progressed into my thirties, during which I built myself a nice life. Some of those friendships solidified, new ones cycled in, I moved to the desert, constructed a home, and then, like an old lover, apricot chicken reared its syrupy head. I went home, six years after moving, almost ten years on from the tiny apartment with the roommate in the closet, and threw a family dinner. I was excited to cook something special for my friends, and for them to get to know one another. There was a new version of me to meet too, replete with bleached hair and clear skin and a penchant for the phrase "Saturn's Return." The crowd was a mixture—new and old friends, people from New York, California, and other countries. Many were meeting for the first time.

I stood at the stove as the first guest arrived—Kashi, a small, formidable woman with butt-length onyx hair and an all-black wardrobe. As she came down the hall of my friend Bryn's loft, she lobbed in her Australian accent, "What's for dinner? Aye-pricot chicken?" I laughed. Only a real friend could pull that reference.

Then Hayden appeared, like a glint off a crystal, suddenly towering over my shoulder, and in her cosmic near-whisper said, "Are we having apricot chicken?" My mouth smiled but my eyes rolled.

By the time Fabiana loped in, I was braced. I beat her to the punch. "What do you think is for dinner, Bobby?" Without a pause: "Apricot chicken." Her staccato laughter peppered me like a burst of Venezuelan gunfire. "You guys! I know how to cook now!" I showed them the delicious offerings on the stove, in the fridge, already on the table. I'd spent years developing past my earliest culinary forays, but I had miscalculated; I thought it would be a tender moment of nostalgia to bring back the old bull. I had wandered blissfully to the slaughter. It took me forty minutes to reveal that in the oven was a hefty rack of none other than everybody's favorite guest star.

That night my friends roasted me. We sat around Bryn's corner windows overlooking the Williamsburg Bridge and Lower Manhattan, and they laughed so hard some of them cried, at my expense, about the many instances of apricot chicken they'd endured. They recounted the time I had to make my own Russian dressing because it was impossible to find; the times I burned it but we had nothing else; the shared horror of discovering what the ingredients were; the times they had to explain to new lovers that this was a rite of passage in our family, not an example of our actual tastes; and ultimately, how so many of those times it was the only meal anyone had cooked for them in such a long time that not only did it give them sustenance, it kept them alive. I learned that night that a roast is my love language, but . . .

I hope every one of you fucks reads this book and hears me say definitively: We may not have a worn leather armchair to come home to every holiday, but when you need something that makes you feel oddly seen, slightly sick, and overwhelmingly loved, I've got some apricot chicken for you in the oven.

MY GRANDMA'S PEANUT BUTTER COOKIES

 Katie Holmes

THE SCENT OF PEANUT BUTTER TAKES ME BACK TO MY grandmother's kitchen. The window that looked out to the pool. The yellow fridge. Her hands gently holding mine in place as we made crisscross marks on the freshly baked cookies with a fork. The beauty and simplicity of being together and making something. And, of course, her kind smile and infectious laughter.

My grandmother lived in a two-bedroom house with a pool for all of her grandchildren. She was married to Fred, my grandfather, and they had five sons, my father being the youngest.

I remember that whenever my grandmother said my dad's name or looked at his face, her face would take on the shape of pure joy. Her excitement flowed through her as she talked at a quick, consistent pace about a range of subjects whose through line was family, community, and church. I liked to sit close by and listen to these exchanges. I would always be very quiet, as though I were sitting on the edge of a harmonious river that glittered under the sun. They shared such goodness and respect for each other. It was easy, and it was calm.

My grandmother always reported joy and never seemed interested in gossip. Maybe she didn't have time to worry about the missteps of others, or maybe she just saw people as fully dimensional and deserving of compassion. I believe it was the latter. To me, she was made of sweetness. Her hands were so warm and so kind when they held my little fingers.

Each of my grandmother's sons had at least five children. I am the youngest of my family and that put me in the place of the youngest grandchild. I loved my cousins so much, but I was very shy and sometimes felt overwhelmed by all of them because they were much older than me. I wasn't quite sure where I was supposed to take up space. But I did enjoy having a special bond with my dad as the youngest.

My grandma was in her early seventies when I was around five years old. She would have me over for a visit and it would be just the two of us. Looking through her thick glasses, she would shine her bright blue eyes on me and smile. She would tell me things like "You are very special" and "You have big eyes, just like mine" when we would sit in her living room together. She would often bring me a special tin of her clip-on earrings and let me borrow them. I didn't have my ears pierced and she knew I liked her earrings. I felt so lucky and touched that she wanted me to have them. It did make me feel very special.

My grandma giggled all the time. Her giggles made me giggle, and before I knew it, I didn't feel so shy. Our time together gave me a place in our family. I was the baby but I was seen, and with my grandma I even got to be a big girl and wear earrings.

Making peanut butter cookies with my grandma was my favorite thing to do. We took it very seriously because we knew that they were very popular in our family. At first, I was only given the job of making the crisscross marks when the cookies came out of the oven. I can still feel her hands helping mine. Eventually, I was given the responsibility of mixing the butter and eggs *and* crisscrossing the newly baked cookies.

When my cousins and I get together, we often talk about our grandma's cookies and then about Grandma. She had this way about her. She knew how to make everyone feel better. You could be having the worst day and Grandma would look at you and say, "You look so nice today. You have the prettiest smile."

Today, whenever I walk past a bakery and smell that scent, I think about my grandma. I remember the power of kindness and compassion. And I think of her beautiful joy. I carry her prayer card in my wallet so that she is with me each time I try a bakery's peanut butter cookie.

I have never found one as good as Grandma's.

Peanut Butter Cookies

1 cup shortening (Crisco) or unsalted butter
1 cup dark brown sugar, packed
1 cup granulated sugar
2 large eggs, beaten
1 teaspoon vanilla
1 cup peanut butter (creamy)
2½ cups all-purpose flour
1 teaspoon baking soda
½ teaspoon baking powder
½ teaspoon salt

Preheat oven to 375°F. Line a baking sheet with parchment paper.

In a large bowl, mix together the shortening, brown sugar, and granulated sugar. Add the eggs, vanilla, and peanut butter. Add the flour, baking soda, baking powder, and salt. Mix the dough very well and then roll into one-inch balls.

Flatten each ball on the lined baking sheet.

Bake for 9 to 10 minutes.

As the cookies cool, make a crisscross mark on each of them with a fork.

These cookies are best eaten with cold milk.

WHAT DO YOU EAT WHEN YOU DON'T EAT?

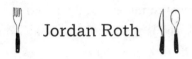 Jordan Roth

HAT DO YOU EAT WHEN YOU DON'T EAT? MINE WAS an apple. The intoxicating power of getting through a whole day on just one. The trick is to cut it slowly into tiny pieces so that in the same time it takes the rest of the cafeteria table to scarf down their entire trays, you have stretched your one perfect apple into a full meal, leaving the rest of your tray untouched. And no one will notice, least of all your stomach.

These are the secret recipes of the anorexic. Strangely called an eating disorder when its brilliance is that it brings order, rules, control, power to the powerless.

I was told I'd never be anorexic. At a checkup when my doctor found out I was starting to skip meals, he said, "You're not gonna be anorexic or anything, but restricting isn't a healthy way to lose weight." *You think I can't do it. You think I'm not strong enough, that I don't have what it takes. Watch me. I'll show you.* That's what I believed from right then in his office at fifteen years old until right now, when writing his words I realized he was just trying not to scare me. Trying not to make it sound too dire. Maybe.

Well, I showed him. Six months later, I showed him every week on his scale for my required weigh-ins. He seemed as helpless then as I had been for all those years of fatness. All he could do was take my blood, report on the latest mineral and vitamin deficiencies, and give me a pep/scare talk about the bad things that would happen in my body next. As if I'd hear them as bad.

Then the scale. I'd watch his finger nudge the black weight as the arrow bobbed up and down. I willed it to sink just a little more. I wanted full credit for my work. And I didn't want approximations. "It's still moving," I'd insist as he inched it lower.

My parents, whom I had also rendered helpless by now, tried their best to keep up, even if they couldn't keep control. My father tried through research. He got the book—there was only one—on males with eating disorders, which declared that there are only two kinds of males with eating disorders: wrestlers and gays. We knew which one I wasn't, but I wasn't interested in being outed by *Males with Eating Disorders*.

My mother tried her best by sitting next to me at the kitchen table to watch me eat and by believing that if only she could find me the right meal, this would all stop. She'd rummage through the mess of take-out menus in the top drawer and race around New York trying to find my glass-slipper food.

For me, it was E.A.T. Literally, a restaurant called E.A.T. Usually an invitation, now a desperate mother's plea. An iconic Upper East Side café with its windows full of Zabar's breads and its expanse of glass cases shielding mounds of salads within is where I spied the white beans. Mushy to the eye yet firm to the mouth, swimming in a stewed mix of cherry tomatoes, garlic, and rosemary. A sidekick to the roast vegetable, goat cheese, and onion sandwich on impossibly thin slices of focaccia.

I didn't always actually eat at E.A.T., but it was my mother's best shot at getting me to take at least a few bites. Sometimes on weekends we'd go there, walking the flour-dusted black-and-white-checkered linoleum path to the too-small bistro tables, where I'd say there was no room for the overflowing bread basket (there wasn't, and not just because I was carb-phobic) and she'd insist there was. Or after school, she'd get takeout, the white beans so stuffed into a plastic container that you couldn't open it without tomato paste oozing down the sides. She'd always try to sneak in one of their famous raisin walnut rolls and get frustrated when I'd pick out the raisins and the walnuts and leave the bread, even though the whole thing was only a two-inch cube.

And then the sandwich. "There's nothing bad in there," she'd implore as I peeled back the top piece of bread looking for land mines. She didn't understand that I already knew it was bad. That all food was bad. That all of me was bad. But just for that moment, I believed her and took a bite. And just for that moment, it felt good.

Eventually, my anorexia moved on. Not because I beat it, but because its work was finished. It had done what it came to do, not against me, but for me. The reasons remained, and still do, but they had been expressed—violently, beautifully expressed—so it moved on. Not gone, never gone, just further away. Like the sun in winter. Still there, just not as hot.

Most diseases are "I haves." "I have the flu," not "I am the flu." This one is "I have" and "I am." I have anorexia, I am anorexic. An "I am" lingers. It is you.

I still eat an apple a day, but now for breakfast, not a whole day. I still cut it into little pieces, but now that's in order to mix it with oatmeal. My mother still tries to find food that fits my latest rules and still tries to get me to eat more of it. E.A.T. is still there, and though I haven't been in years, it's good to know, just in case.

HOT CROSS BUNS

 Leanne Shapton

I WAS PREGNANT, AND I WAS SICK. NAUSEA, MORNING SICK-
ness, call it what you like. It had come on suddenly one day while I
was riding in the passenger seat of our car. I asked my then-husband
to pull over on a country road so I could heave.

From that day on, the urge to barf was there. Ever present. Like a
little ghost sitting between my gut and glottis.

One thing that would help, other than being unconscious, was
dough. Up until then, I had no cravings, but the sickness had me craving carbs, bread, "stodge," the English call it.

I also had a subchorionic hematoma, which meant losing the fetus
was a likelihood.

It was June when I found out I was pregnant. I'd been in Rome
the week before with a friend, her mother, and her sister. I roamed
with these women, drinking fizzy water and blood orange San Pel-
legrino, avoiding wine, thinking of Christians, slaves, and empire. We
saw Proserpina raped, Daphne and Apollo, the Vatican. I watched my

friend and her mother on that trip to Rome. I loved how they were affectionate with each other, how they pushed their sunglasses over their blond hair and draped scarves over their arms and shoulders.

I also saw a wooden painted St. Anthony, the patron saint of lost things, in the window of a junk shop. About eight inches tall. He was worn, robes faded. There was something about him. He reminded me of my suburban Catholic elementary school, the statue of the Virgin Mary in the foyer, my fear of the crucifix, and the art of the German artist Paloma Varga Weisz. He also reminded me of a ship's figurehead. (I've always been spooked by those whittled, painted souls on the prows of ships, so exposed, so lonely and fixed.)

The shop was closed when I saw the figure, when we walked past it on the way to dinner somewhere. There were no store hours on the door. I remember eating pasta with liver that night. I made it a point to walk by the shop whenever I could during our few remaining days in Rome, to see if it ever opened. It never did.

The morning of the day I left Rome, I visited a flea market in Trastevere. I found two vases and a black-and-white boned silk dress from the fifties. When I passed the little junk shop one last time, it was still closed.

Over the next few months, the dress grew tighter as the fetus grew bigger and my nausea grew sharper. I ate buns, and toast, and little cranberry walnut rolls. When the hematoma was detected at about seven weeks, my obstetrician warned me not to lift anything more than five pounds. Said not to swim in ponds; said if I had to travel, to nap where and when I could. "If you're going to lose the baby, you're going to lose the baby," my doctor said, "but staying home in bed won't change anything."

This was the summer of 2012. I'd been asked by a Canadian magazine to write about the swimming events at the London Olympics. My doctor said I should go but to take it easy. "Don't do anything stupid." I called my friend Craig and asked him to meet me at Paddington Station so he could help me with my suitcase. "I'm pregnant and it's complicated," I told him. At that point, I'd told only three people.

I stayed with Craig and Debby on the edge of Hampstead Heath, not far from the overland train that would take me to the Olympic Park and Zaha Hadid's maxi-pad-resemblant pool. On the way to and from the station, I'd pass a Marks & Spencer food market. I knew from previous family visits that in England, hot cross buns could be found year-round, despite Queen Elizabeth I's decree that they be baked and sold only on Good Friday, Christmas, and for burials. So there I found, even in July, six-packs of soft, glowing hot cross buns. They were my little heath-side Lourdes.

I love a hot cross bun, always have. In the suburb of Toronto where I grew up, they'd appear around Easter, then vanish. On some versions, the cross would be sugar icing, yay; on others, bland pastry dough, boo.

HOT CROSS BUNS

But the studs of dried fruit, the greenish citron, the peel, the spices (which are said to represent the spices laid on the dead body of Christ at burial), the joy. Our family bought and ate day-old bread.

That summer, the buns, when I could get them, were truly a holiday.

I brought my buns to the Olympics. I ate them as I watched Michael Phelps win more gold medals. Watched the poorer countries win none. Between events, I went to the infirmary, explained my situation, and took a nap on a cot. When I woke, I'd drink milky tea, eat a hot cross bun, and go back to the pool.

Mit bun was the only way I could function in London. I'd tell friends to meet me outside Greggs, a bakery chain, instead of the pub. I'd walk around with hot-cross-bun crumbs down the front of my dresses, caught on the minor swell. Always, always worrying about the tenuous hold this bun in my oven had on life. If I was jostled by a bus ride or grew tired from some little exertion, I'd tense, dread, go home. Every time I used the toilet, I braced myself for blood. Then I'd pull up my underpants, sit on the bed in my room, the rest of the house quiet, and eat another bun to keep from vomiting.

I don't think I realized all the symbolism and metaphor piped onto this trimester. The prayer came into my mouth, not out of it.

A few weeks later, the hematoma had absorbed, the pregnancy was progressing normally, my nausea ebbed, ended. I think of St. Anthony before I lose things.

My daughter plays the wobbling notes on her cream-colored recorder.

Hot. Cross. Buns. Hot. Cross. Buns. One. A. Pen. Ny. Two. A Pen. Ny. Hot. Cross. Buns.

When I make hot cross buns, I use this adaptation of a recipe by Dan Lepard:

Hot Cross Buns

FOR THE BUNS:

⅔ cup (150 ml) beer at room temperature (such as brown ale)
1 ¼-ounce package fast-action yeast
½ cup plus 1 tablespoon (75 g) whole wheat flour
⅔ cup (150 g) half-and-half
4 teaspoons mixed spices, such as pumpkin pie spice mix
2 medium eggs
⅓ cup (50 g) light brown sugar, packed, or honey
1⅔ cups (300 g) mixed raisins, currants, citron, glacé cherries, dried
  cranberries, and/or dried fruit
1 tablespoon Branston pickle
Zest of 1 orange
3 cups (400 g) all-purpose flour
2½ tablespoons (25 g) corn flour
1 teaspoon salt
Oil for kneading

FOR THE CROSS:

1¼ cups (150 g) all-purpose flour
3 tablespoons plus 1 teaspoon (50 ml) sunflower oil
½ cup (125 ml) water
1 beaten egg for glaze
Demerara sugar

Mix the beer, yeast, and whole wheat flour in a bowl, and leave to
bubble for 30 minutes. In a saucepan, put the half-and-half, mixed
spices, eggs, and sugar or honey over low heat and stir until just warm,
about blood heat. Pour into the yeast mix and add the dried fruit,
pickle, and zest. In another bowl, stir the flour, corn flour, and salt, then
add the yeast mixture to it. Combine to a soft, sticky dough and leave
for 10 minutes.

Lightly oil a work surface, and gently knead the dough for 10 seconds. Return the dough to the bowl, then cover and leave somewhere warm for an hour, until risen slightly. Divide into 12 roughly 3½-ounce (100-g) pieces, shape into balls, and put on a tray lined with nonstick paper. Cover and leave to rise somewhere warm until almost doubled.

Mix the cross ingredients and spoon into a piping bag with a plain ⅓-inch (¾-cm) nozzle.

Heat the oven to 425°F, pipe crosses on the buns, brush with egg, sprinkle with sugar, and bake for 15 to 18 minutes. Remove from the oven and leave until almost cool.

SAFTA DALIA-INSPIRED FLAVORFUL ROAST DRUMSTICKS

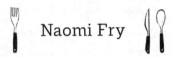 Naomi Fry

T HE HOME I GREW UP IN WAS A GOOD ONE: SAFE AND secure and organized. My parents provided me and my older sister with a functional and predictable life: we went to sleep at the same time every night and rose at the same time every morning; we were reminded to do our homework and asked how we did on our tests; our clothes were always laundered and our nails were always clean; and as far as nutrition went, my mother made us healthy and balanced meals, heavy on vegetables and whole grains and light on salt and oil and sugar. It's pretty much a given that this sort of life has endless upsides, but we often crave what we lack, and as a child, I craved just a little bit of irregularity, a little bit of edge.

What I craved, in a word, was flavor. When it came to food, this hankering was literal, and I took flavor wherever I could get it. I bought and consumed treats both salty and sweet after school, before I reached my house (tangy, oily potato chips; vanilla ice cream bars dipped in brittle chocolate; Bissli, a pasta-shaped snack offered in my native Israel in a variety of intense seasonings, whose name translates, literally, to "a bite for me"). I ate dishes cooked by friends' mothers that, because of their decadently high fat content, would have never been made by my own. (Especially memorable is a medium-rare steak swimming in a red wine and cream sauce I had one night, a specialty of one ex-boyfriend's mom.) And at my maternal grandmother's, I ate roast chicken.

My mother made chicken too, but in her desire to eschew the greasy, unpredictably spreading smells of cooking, the bird came out of the oven barely a shade or two darker than it had been when it went in. I could eat it, but I certainly didn't crave it. I loved my mother—she meant only the best!—but I didn't love her chicken. My grandmother's chicken, however, was something else entirely. In Safta Dalia's house (*safta* means "grandma" in Hebrew), even the provisions were more fun, less bland, than in our own home. There, my sister and I sucked on sugar cubes, which were stored in an old jam jar; we ate slice after slice of spicy salami; we nibbled on savory olives. And though Safta Dalia didn't cook many things, what she did cook, she cooked with commitment. When her chicken came out of the oven, it was browned, the skin glazed and crackling. It wasn't seasoned with anything more than salt and maybe pepper, I don't think, but to me, that was enough. I would ask for a drumstick and tear into it, the meat tender and moist beneath the chicken's papery skin. My hands would get oily, as would my face, but I really didn't care.

NAOMI FRY

The recipe I chose to share isn't my grandmother's. I never found out how she made her chicken, and now, sadly, it's too late. But it *is* a recipe for an easy-to-make roast chicken that is flavorful and satisfyingly crispy. (I use drumsticks, still my favorite part of the bird, and to the salt and pepper I also add sumac, one of my favorite spices.) I am now also a mom, and my house, I hope for the sake of my daughter, is safe and secure and organized. But every once in a while, I also like to have a little bit of flavor.

Flavorful Roast Drumsticks

YIELD: 4 TO 6 SERVINGS

Time: 1 hour and 45 minutes

INGREDIENTS

12 chicken drumsticks, skin on
Salt and pepper, to taste
Sumac, to taste
Olive oil, to taste

PREPARATION

Heat oven to 425°F.

Line a baking dish with aluminum foil and place the drumsticks on it in a single layer. Sprinkle liberally with salt, pepper, and sumac, and drizzle generously with olive oil.

Put the baking dish in the oven, uncovered, and roast until the drumsticks are browned (about 1 hour and 45 minutes). If you'd like, you can add some chunks of peeled potatoes to the dish and they will taste very nice alongside the chicken.

Serve and enjoy!

SANCOCHO DREAMING!

 John Leguizamo

S ANCOCHO IS THE SOUP OF THE CARIBBEAN, OF COLOMBI-
ans, Dominicans, Puerto Ricans, Cubans, Hondurans, Ecuador-
ians, Panamanians, and Venezuelans. Central Americans have
it too, but they call it by a different name (sopas). But wherever you're
from, it's a hearty soup, and it has to be full of flavor. It's the Latin
penicillin—it will cure whatever ails ya.

Sancocho comes from the Spanish verb *sancochar*, which means to
parboil. It's a very primordial dish. It's a very Latin dish. And it's a national dish. But it's also a dish of revolution. It's representative of our
culture. It's the mixture of our white, Black, and Indigenous blood. It's
the ruins of our powerful empires. It's the stock of our near genocide.
It's what's left after the robbery of all our wealth. If you go to Europe,
you can see the splendor of their cities, built with our countries' stolen
riches: 181 tons of our gold and 16,000 tons of our silver were taken.

The size of the Empire State Building. But at least we still have our sancocho.

Sancocho may take hours to make, but the flavor will seep into your soul forever. Get some speakers, put on some Fania salsa or La Sonora Matancera in the background, and you'll be transported to a magical setting straight out of a Gabriel García Márquez novel.

The soup always reminds me of the countryside in Colombia, where everyone is so generous and every ingredient is natural and organic. They only use free-range chickens. And when I say *free-range*, I mean *OG* free-range. I'm talking about chickens so free that they run around the farm and dodge trucks on the highway and never get hit. The sancocho host gets their vegetables from their own private gardens, which are huge compared to American yards. Then they use real wood-burning fires and giant clay pots to cook. It's not like Joe Schmoe and a grill from Home Depot—it's a full-on bonfire.

I had this soup after the death of my grandfather. We sat around as we ate the stew and told stories of his life, his accomplishments, of the great man he had been. Nobody happened to mention that he also stole my parents' savings to pay off his own debt, leaving them impoverished. Nobody brought up how the stress of our family's financial situation wrecked my mother and father's marriage. Nobody cared to discuss that I have compounded trauma and a paranoia of being robbed. Nobody talked about any of these things. But at least we still had our sancocho.

Then there was the time when we sipped the soup with family I had never met before, deep in the jungle. They were the most gracious hosts, and they made the best-tasting sancocho I ever had. It was almost a perfect meal, but ironically, as we ate, the mosquitoes ate us alive. After, our skin looked like the outside of a pineapple. Bumpy and lumpy and rough from the mosquito assault. The pain was legendary. I was slapping myself so much it almost had a Biggie Smalls beat, *"Biggie, Biggie, can't you see? Sometimes your words just hypnotize me. . . . That's why they broke and you're so paid."* Those welts would take weeks to stop itching. But at least we had our sancocho.

Or when I was in Cartagena near García Márquez's main hangout and we started telling raunchy tales of failed sexual escapades. Ribbing one another on our own and others' physical and intellectual frailties . . . very Colombian to be a kidder. The laughs were abundant and the storytelling prevailed for hours into the night. And we had our sancocho.

Then there was the time in Cali on tour . . .

Then there was the time filming on location in Miami . . .

Sancocho doesn't just feed my soul. It has a soul of its own. When I'm feeling diminished in America, I make sancocho to feel culturally replenished. So I can be a warrior and help move America one cultural evolutionary notch forward. Because even though I may face invisible quotas, stingy tokenism, and hidden glass ceilings, one thought always comforts me: At least I have my sancocho.

Sancocho

Note: Moms are mad proud and protective of their secret "sancocho tweaks." So any additions or subtractions you choose will make it even more fun.

- ½ garlic bulb
- 2 bunches scallions or spring onions
- 2 bunches fresh cilantro
- 3 medium-size green plantains
- 5 tablespoons olive oil
- ½ teaspoon white pepper
- ½ teaspoon ground cumin
- 5 pounds beef ribs (Tell your butcher to cut the ribs in half and to cut off some of the fat.)
- 1 pound frozen yucca (You can find it in a 2-pound bag.)
- One 16-ounce bag of frozen arracacha (yellow cassava) (Arracacha is a root from the Andes used by Incan and Arawak tribes; buy it frozen in your local bodega or Spanish food store.)
- 4 large potatoes
- 2 teaspoons salt, to taste

FIRST PROCESS

Mince the garlic.

Finely chop the scallions (whole stem and root).

Rinse half a bunch of cilantro (leave full stems).

Peel the green plantains, slice lengthwise into quarters, then chop into thirds.

In a pressure cooker, put 5 tablespoons of olive oil and set at low heat.

Add garlic and scallions and sauté for 3 minutes. Watch and stir.

Add cilantro and sauté for another 3 minutes.

Add ½ teaspoon of white pepper.

Add ½ teaspoon of cumin.

Add ribs and sauté for 3 or 4 minutes on each side.

Add green plantains.

Add water to the pressure cooker; it should fill about two-thirds of the pot.

Raise heat from medium to high heat.

Cook for 25 minutes in a closed pressure cooker. After the 25 minutes, turn off the flame on the stove and let the pressure cooker rest for a few minutes, then release the pressure/steam manually.

SECOND PROCESS

Into a separate large soup pot, pour the contents of the pressure cooker.

Add yucca as is from the frozen bag.

Add arracacha as is from the bag.

Peel the potatoes, then cut into eighths.

Add the potatoes.

Add one-quarter of the remaining half of the first bunch of cilantro.

Add more cilantro, garlic, or scallions to taste.

Add white pepper and salt to taste.

Add water till the soup pot is three-quarters filled.

Cook at medium heat for 20 minutes.

Serve the sancocho with rice and avocado.

Add the rest of the chopped cilantro as a garnish at end.

GRAMMA'S KITCHEN

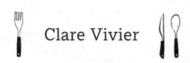 Clare Vivier

I HAVE ENJOYED MANY EXTRAORDINARY MEALS IN MY LIFE, but some of my most memorable are the ones from my childhood made by my grandma. These were not fancy or decadent meals— they were made with just a few simple ingredients, and I'll never forget them.

My parents grew up in a small town in Indiana. My father's parents had both migrated here from Mexico as children with their families. Frances Castillo and Nicholas Guerrero, my grandparents, eventually met and started a family of their own, and my dad was the third of nine kids.

My parents would take us children back to Indiana every summer to see family. My favorite place to be was Gramma Guerrero's house, or specifically, her kitchen, where we'd find her dressed in one of her homemade floral housecoats, working away, preparing food to welcome her visiting family. Her house always smelled like fresh tortillas, pinto beans, and rice cooking on the stove.

Gramma made only flour tortillas, never corn. Maybe this was because she was from Monterrey, Mexico—a northern region of the country where flour tortillas were slightly more common than in other regions—but more likely it was because the masa needed to make corn tortillas was not something she could easily find in Indiana in the 1930s, so she used what she could. We loved her tortillas—they were very thin, white discs, lightly spotted with scorch marks from where the bubbles would touch the flat cast-iron griddle. She'd flip it with her bare hands and wait for the remaining dough to turn from transparent to an opaque white before she'd snatch it off the fire and toss it with the others onto a soft and threadbare plaid kitchen towel. At Gramma's house, we didn't eat with forks—utensils were rarely even put on the table—just a stack of freshly made tortillas wrapped in a folded dish towel in the center of the table. And next to that was a bowl of her homemade salsa, which she called "chile." We'd take a warm fresh tortilla, rip off a piece, and pick up the chile-covered beans and rice.

My grandpa worked at the foundry, and to feed nine kids on that kind of wage was not easy; my grandma had to find ways to feed them all on what she had available. Every day for lunch, my dad and his siblings ate bean "tacos." They were homemade flour tortillas folded in half with a layer of smashed pinto beans like a chunky spread, with a dab of her chile. Gramma would make stacks of these tacos and put them in plastic bags in the freezer to be doled out to her kids. My dad used to tell me stories about going to work in the fields to pick crops during the summer. He said those bean taco lunches were always the best part of his day. Throughout her life, my grandmother continued to make these tacos, always keeping a stash of them in her freezer.

These tacos were the perfect combination of buttery, chewy tortilla with beans, and a hint of tomato, onion, and jalapeños from her salsa. It's that simple perfect combination of flour, fat, water, and salt topped with a savory protein and a little acidity.

Each year, when we were about to leave Indiana for the summer and embark upon the drive back to Minnesota, my grandma would get up early to make us food for the road. She would load us up with a few bags filled with still-warm bean tacos, and it almost made the twelve-hour station-wagon ride with my parents and five siblings tolerable.

When my grandma died several years ago, someone found a zip-lock bag containing her last stack of bean tacos in the freezer, and a family feud almost erupted over who got to enjoy them.

My cousins recorded my grandma's recipes, so now we can all re-create her food. It's always a hit with friends, but for me, nothing will compare with eating Gramma's tortillas fresh off the griddle and made with love.

BURNT TOAST TO THE OLD LIFE

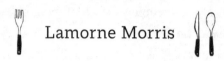

Lamorne Morris

I 'M WRITING THIS ESSAY WHILE I SIT IN ISOLATION DUE TO complications from COVID-19. Besides the normal aches and pains this virus brings, it hasn't been so bad for me. Let me explain. COVID is bad. It sucks. But having ten days to gather my thoughts and relax isn't a raw deal. One of the perks is that I get to watch whatever I want, whenever I want. (The new season of *Woke* on Hulu is FIRE!) But my favorite perk, and perhaps most important, is that I get to order whatever food I want. That's right, I have access to any and every meal in the city thanks to delivery apps like Uber Eats and DoorDash. But herein lies the culinary quagmire: food just doesn't taste as great when you're in isolation. I realized that no matter how much I enjoy truffle fries, they just aren't the same without a little ambience to go along with them.

That's when it hit me, I'm not obsessed with great food, I'm obsessed with the environment in which I eat said great food.

Years back I used to wait tables at a place in Chicago called Ed Debevic's. I worked in the suburban location, but whatever, bro. Same thing . . . kinda. Well, if you've never been to Ed's, then you are truly missing out. The menu is simple: burgers, fries, milkshakes, beer, etc. With such a simple menu, one could ask, how come this place is always packed from wall to wall? Simple answer: Ed's is a PARTY! People don't come to Ed's for the food, they come for the service and the environment. When I worked there, I was allowed to eat people's food, curse them out, sing karaoke, and completely ignore the guests for an entire shift. The place is a dream for young actors trying to make money. But more important, it's a place to have fun!

I didn't quite understand why my love for food was the way it was until this week of isolation. Turns out, I love people! I love truffle fries as much as the next person, but they don't taste as great without a bourbon old-fashioned and some live music to accompany them. There's something about appealing to *all* of your senses while enjoying a delicious meal. I get to taste the burger, look at all the pretty people, feel the sticky floor, smell the aromas of bathrooms that I'm in proximity to, all while some smooth jazz tantalizes my ears. That's a great night out.

Food is great for the soul, sure. But the magic ingredient to any recipe is enjoying that food with the folks you love in a place you love, sticky floors and all.

EATING YOUR IDENTITY

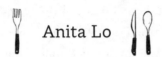

Anita Lo

I HAVE A LOVE-HATE RELATIONSHIP WITH DUMPLINGS.

On one hand, what's not to love? A well-made dumpling is like a beautifully wrapped gift—cute little purses of deliciousness, comfort food at its finest. Dim sum is one of my favorite ways to pass an afternoon, although the situation with the carts stresses me out. I love dumplings so much that I feel I have to be vigilant at all times lest I miss out on one.

Growing up, we used to make them as a family on occasional Sunday mornings. My mother would make and roll out the wrappers, and my siblings and I would fold them. It was a fun, crafty event that always ended with a satisfying lunch, and it was one of the finite number of fond family memories that I have.

Later, as a professional chef, I drew on those experiences and created what became my signature dish: foie gras soup dumplings with jicama and a black vinegar reduction. And then later I consulted on a fast-casual dumpling restaurant in the early aughts.

And then the dumpling swallowed me.

As a chef of color, I am constantly being pigeonholed. I am firmly French trained—I went to cooking school in France, I worked at Bouley and at Chanterelle, and I have even been knighted by the French government with the Order of Agricultural Merit. Plus I had a contemporary American restaurant for seventeen years that brought in influences from all over the world. Yet I am quite often expected to do only Asian-inflected cuisine. And it's not even about my heritage. I'm Chinese, but any Asian influence will do.

Then there is the pigeonholing within the pigeonholing. Somewhere, someone has dubbed me the go-to dumpling ambassador. My public persona is handcuffed to a dumpling. Confined in a white, doughy exterior, my inner complexity isn't allowed to shine through. Do I look like a dumpling? Okay, I'm pudgy and appear pleated in places, but how did this bite come to define me? I'm actually no dumpling expert. I can make any number of tasty fillings, but my dough is just good enough. And I prefer the standard pork-and-chive dumplings that I can buy in Chinatown to my own.

In the beginning, I had my restaurant Annisa to promote, so any media exposure, for the most part, was necessary, dumpling-focused publicity included. I'm not sure exactly when that started to get old. But I've become more aware of my frustration over time—

how it grows each time someone just assumes I'm going to teach a dumpling class, how it resurfaces during the inevitable yearly asks around Chinese New Year and AAPI heritage month, and how it sits with me during the silence in between.

This past year has been a particularly fraught dumpling year. With the rise of anti-Chinese rhetoric stemming from the last administration, I've felt the need to represent the Chinese part of my identity proudly. So when the dumpling requests came around, I've mostly said yes. But when the ask was specifically framed as a response to anti-Asian violence by a well-meaning charity for their employees, I declined. In that context, it felt like an exercise in assuaging guilt and fell way short. Yet I've still felt like an Uncle Tong with every other dumpling request. Is the dumpling not just a culinary trope for Asian-ness? Is it not unlike the kung fu of the food world? Still, I do love making them, and the effort sometimes supports a good cause or results in a nice paycheck.

So it's not without self-consciousness that I'm offering you a dumpling recipe. It's ironic and it's complicated. Pretty much how I feel about dumplings.

Here is a recipe for banana dumplings—yellow on the outside, white on the inside. Chinese, yet not Chinese. Complex and formed from a multitude of cultural influences. You look at it and it is just another dumpling among the endless varieties out there—unseen until you actually take a bite and look inside.

Banana Dumplings

INGREDIENTS

DOUGH:

    1¼ cups (125 g) all-purpose flour, plus more for dusting
    1 large egg plus one large egg yolk
    1 tablespoon sugar
    1 large pinch kosher salt

FILLING:

    3 ripe bananas, mashed (about 1½ cups)
    1 tablespoon mascarpone
    1 egg white, lightly beaten
    2 tablespoons white sesame seeds
    ¼ cup jicama, cut into small dice
    3 tablespoons sugar
    Pinch salt

DIPPING SAUCE:

    ½ cup water
    ⅓ cup sugar
    ⅓ cup cocoa powder
    Pinch ground cinnamon
    Pinch fruity chili powder such as cobanero
    Pinch salt
    Dash pure vanilla extract

METHOD

Make the dough (or substitute store-bought, yellow dumpling wrappers): Place the flour on a clean surface and form a well in the center. Add to the well the egg and egg yolk plus the sugar and salt. Beat the egg with a fork, then slowly mix in the flour from the sides, without breaking the well walls, until you have a paste. Then you can break the wall and mix in the rest. Knead until smooth and bouncy, about 8 minutes. Cover with plastic wrap and set aside while you make the filling.

Make the filling: Mix all ingredients together until well combined. When the dough has rested at least 30 minutes, roll into a thick rectangle with a rolling pin, then fold in thirds lengthwise to form a square. Roll again into a rectangle to make the folded edges the longer sides. Then use a pasta machine, starting at setting #1 and incrementally rolling until you get to #6, dusting the dough in between. You will need to cut it in half at some point when the dough gets too long. Use a 3- to 3.5-inch round biscuit cutter to make the wrappers.

Fill the wrappers: Place a heaping tablespoon of filling in the center of a wrapper. Fold up each side around the filling to make a taco shape. Starting at one end, make small pleats on the wrapper side that faces you (wet the edges, if needed, to help make a seal). The other, farther side should stay flat. Pinch the pleat from the front to the straight back side and repeat, making equidistant pleats, until you reach the other end. You should have a crescent shape, with the pleated side curving outward. Place on a sheet pan dusted with flour and cover with a damp cloth. Repeat until all the filling is used. At this point you can either cook the dumplings right away or freeze them right on the tray, then transfer to a ziplock bag once frozen. Cook them from the frozen state—do not defrost.

Make the dipping sauce: Place all ingredients except for the vanilla in a saucepan and, over medium heat, slowly bring to a simmer, whisking until it thickens slightly and is of uniform consistency. Stir in the vanilla.

To cook: You can either steam the dumplings—5 minutes if fresh, 6 minutes if frozen—or panfry. To panfry, heat a nonstick pan on high. Add a few tablespoons of a neutral oil, such as canola, and swirl to coat the bottom of the pan. Add the dumplings, crest sides up. Fill the pan halfway up the sides of the dumplings with water, and cover. Turn the heat to medium to medium high and cook until the water is evaporated and the bottoms of the dumplings are golden brown and crispy.

Serve both the dumplings and the dipping sauce hot.

WHITE VANS AND COOKIE SALAD

 Matt Flanders

S A CHILD, I FANTASIZED ABOUT BEING KIDNAPPED. I heard that kidnappers drove white vans, so whenever I saw one, I'd wave frantically and try to look my cutest—that usually involved a knock-kneed stance and a slightly tilted baseball cap like I'd seen on some child model in a JCPenney ad. To be clear, I didn't know what being kidnapped meant exactly. I just knew it involved going somewhere else.

I was never quite satisfied with home. Two-year-old me would tell my grandmother I was running away and toddle off into the woods behind our house in Juneau, Alaska. Nanny, as we called her, would warn me about the wolves and then sneak upstairs and howl out the open windows, sending me scrambling back. But I wouldn't stay put long. Nanny once got a call from someone at the bank where my dad worked letting her know that he was away at a meeting and I was standing there in his office. I'd braved the wolves and walked there on my own while she thought I was napping.

My wanderlust only intensified when we moved to Montana, which is where my obsession with getting kidnapped began. Helena, Montana, was a veritable tropical paradise compared to Alaska, so I lived outside. Let me just say, there were a lot of white vans out there in the 1970s. My arms ache thinking about all that damn waving. But once I realized kidnappings didn't happen as often as I'd hoped, I hatched another plan. My third-grade girlfriend, Joy, and I arranged to meet at Cunningham Park and hike up to Devil's Kitchen, a cave on nearby Mount Helena. We were going to live there for the rest of our days. But after three hours (kid time) or fifteen minutes (adult human time), I realized that Joy wasn't going to show up, which was probably best because I had packed only my sister's Wonder Woman slumber bag and four Cup O' Noodles. I tried eating one while I waited for her, but it was a grim endeavor with no hot water.

When I reached high school, I finally came up with the perfect escape route. I applied for a foreign exchange program, but my parents were not having any of it. I was a late bloomer, and although I would be sixteen before I left, I looked like I was still in junior high. The fact that I hadn't hit puberty came in handy, however. When I turned in my application and the program administrators wanted to ask my parents some questions, I just pretended I was my mom. My high-pitched voice was often mistaken for hers when people called the house, so why not? I was accepted to the program and assigned a family in . . . wait for it . . . Paris fucking France. I begged and begged to be allowed to go, and my parents relented. I'll never forget the shock and terror on my dad's face as he watched his little boy board that plane. I felt really bad . . . for, like, two minutes.

Paris is where I learned that all lettuces are not iceberg. I saw and tasted a kiwi for the first time. A mango. Real butter. Soft cheese that didn't come in a wrapper. Vegetables that weren't boiled. Tender meat drizzled with sauces so delicious that every drop *had* to be soaked up with fresh bread. Oh, the bread. And a fresh strawberry tart that made me who I am today. While I was abroad, I also became fluent in French; found incredible confidence in myself; traveled throughout Europe; gained six inches and forty pounds; grew my hair out to my chin; and started sporting suave stubble, blue-and-white-striped shirts, chunky European boots, and a leather (!) knapsack. But let's go back to the tart. Sweet Jesus, that tart.

And so it was quite a shock when I returned to Montana to finish up high school. I hadn't been aware of just how bad the food was there until I got home. My mother is not a chef. Her go-to menu items were packaged—shell-shaped pasta with canned tuna, cream of mushroom soup, orange cheese, spaghetti with sauce from a jar and ground beef, and tacos made with yellow packets of seasoning—mild, of course. Oh, and as I mentioned before, boiled vegetables. How did she not know how delicious Brussels sprouts could be if she'd just tossed them in some olive oil, salt, and pepper and roasted them? She may read this, so I'm going to stop there. And to be fair, the woman worked her ass off. She owned a successful bookstore, and she built that business herself. After a long day at work, she needed quick and easy recipes for her family of five. Look, I'm incredibly proud of my mom and all she has accomplished. Now that she's retired, she's become quite a good cook and makes a really solid pie. But back then, and after France, mealtime at the Flanders house was rough.

Before I came out as gay, I brought my college girlfriend home for Thanksgiving. We were grocery shopping, and we passed a display of Durkee French Fried Onions. My girlfriend, who was hilarious and from a very nice Los Angeles family, pondered, "Who actually makes that grody green bean casserole with these things baked on top?" My mom, who had been reaching for them at that moment, slowly lowered her hand and gave me a wink.

We may not have had green bean casserole that Thanksgiving, but there was no chance Mom wasn't going to make a family favorite—cookie salad! This is a recipe she got from my grandma Sylvia after she served it at her house in North Dakota one summer, and we all ate it up like a bunch of wild dogs. I should clarify something. My sisters and I didn't have our first cookie salad in Grandma Sylvia's house exactly. We were in the garage because kids weren't allowed to eat in the house, despite the plastic furniture and rug covers everywhere. It was a nice garage though, and Grandpa George set up a picnic table on some blue Astroturf for us.

Salad is a very different thing in Montana. When you order one at a restaurant, nine times out of ten it comes from a bag with some sad strands of grated carrots and cabbage. Very likely it will also have some sort of meat, cheese, and ranch dressing on top. But cookie salad has none of those things. It's this sort of treacly, ambrosia-type concoction made of pudding, whipped cream, and canned mandarin oranges and pineapple. What?! I can feel that disapproving expression on your face. It's a salad! There's produce in it. And for that crunch you're craving when you ask for a salad, Keebler Fudge Stripes cookies are crumbled on top.

My husband, Will, is from Greenwich, Connecticut—land of the super-WASPs. His family's holiday salad includes crisp butter lettuce, carefully peeled and sliced grapefruit, fresh avocado, pomegranate seeds, and a delicious, top-secret dressing. When he first experienced cookie salad, I saw a perplexed look on his face that I'd never seen before. I honestly feared he might be having a stroke. Alas, he survived, and although he didn't go back for seconds, like the rest of the family, and had many, many questions afterward, he ate his entire portion. It was right then that I knew I'd picked the right guy.

Will works in the luxury travel industry, and I've done some big movies in exotic international locations. We have truly seen the world and eaten the best food in it. I have lived between New York and Los Angeles for more than twenty-five years now, and urban life suits me— the arts, the culture, the liberal politics, the freedom that comes with a certain anonymity, the restaurants—all of it. When I'm back in Montana on one of my frequent visits, I often hear comments about my "fancy" life. It makes me cringe. Yes, I've seen and done and tasted a lot. My life is different from many Montanans', but fancy I am not. I know where and who I come from. I love where and who I come from. And even more than that fresh strawberry tart from a Parisian boulangerie on Rue du Cherche-Midi, I love cookie salad. It's not so much about what it tastes like, but who made it and who I enjoy it with. When I'm surrounded by family and my mom serves me up a huge dollop, I savor each and every bite. Because I have finally come to realize that nothing is sweeter than being home.

Cookie Salad

INGREDIENTS

7 ounces instant vanilla pudding mix
2 cups milk
16 ounces frozen whipped topping, thawed
22 ounces mandarin oranges, drained
20 ounces crushed pineapple, drained
25 Fudge Stripes cookies

INSTRUCTIONS

In a large bowl, combine the vanilla pudding mix and the milk.

Mix until thick.

Fold in the whipped topping.

Stir in the mandarin oranges and crushed pineapple.

Keep chilled at least two hours.

Crumble the cookies on top before serving.

Note: If you have extra marshmallows from your post–snowman-building hot cocoa or after making a giant cornflakes Christmas wreath, go ahead and throw some of those in too.

MEATBALLS

 Danny Sangra

DESPITE THIS BEING A STORY ABOUT LOWLY MEATBALLS, I have to open with what feels like a movie pitch by a group of producers hungry for awards season. The genre: riches-to-rags story. The players: a single mother and her five-year-old child. The setting: a council estate. The soundtrack: New Romantics.

For the first four years of my life, things were good. Better than good. Eighties good. Yes, the early eighties were a grim wasteland of TV dinners and frozen pizza, but that was the low; the high was pure unadulterated excess: big family gatherings, a sports car, various bits of tech to make life more entertaining, and, most important, a big fancy hi-fi.

But then my parents divorced and went bankrupt. Most likely it was this type of excessive pendulum swing that caused the bankruptcy, though I didn't know this at the time. What I do remember is going from a big house, toys, and two parents to one parent, no toys, and living with my grandma. I remember her brown, orange, and cream foldout sofa bed. A cabinet of colored-glass trinkets I was not allowed to play with. She grew rhubarb outside her living room window, and once I got a couple of action figures, the rhubarb became their jungle setting for countless adventures.

My mum and I were left with nothing. Less than nothing. Yet she found a way to survive and managed to find a place for us to live.

We settled in pretty quickly. She wallpapered my room with a primary-colored train pattern and my duvet was covered in the characters from *Fantasia*. We rented a TV that was on a timer, so you'd have to use one-pound coins to keep it going. Our neighbor showed us how to break into the coin box and keep using the same coin. Everything was about surviving without feeling like you were drowning. Weirdly, it felt fun; everything was a hustle and it was all about little victories. Looking back, I know this was the worst time in my mum's life. She probably hates that I'm even writing about it, but it has clearly made me who I am.

My mum was a hairdresser and found a job across the city. This meant that when I started school, she'd walk me there in the morning, then walk to the bus that would get her across the city to work. She'd skip her lunch in order to get back early enough to pick me up (I wouldn't find out about this until I got older).

I'd spend my Saturdays with my auntie or one of my grandmas. When I was with the Jewish side of my family, there would be chicken soup, lokshen, and kneidlach. My dad's side was Sikh, so when I stayed with my other grandma, the food was still chicken, but it was spicy and came with chapati or paratha. I mainly remember my grandma making popcorn and lifting the pan lid because I was curious about what would happen to the kernels when set free.

Sundays, it was just me and my mum. She'd open all the windows while she cleaned the house, typically blasting Motown records. I'd watch cartoons while a chilly, and sort of refreshing, UK morning breeze ran through our home. *Land of the Giants* would come on, followed by *The Waltons*. *The Waltons* was my cue to turn the TV off and go play. My mum would prepare my school clothes and do the washing while making me lunch. I knew Sundays were coming to an end when I'd have a bath and dry in front of the fire while *The A-Team* was on TV.

As this was happening, my mum was preparing dinner. Every Sunday it was the same thing: meatballs. Big gravy-covered meatballs.

I hated them.

The meatballs were the size of a Wiffle ball. I don't know why I'm using a Wiffle ball as my choice of scale, as I don't recall having Wiffle balls in the UK when I was younger. Also, I was much smaller when I was five, so most likely the meatballs were smaller than I remember. Regardless, they seemed massive, and what made it worse was the fact that they disgusted me.

I'd sit at the table and stare at the meatballs. I can't remember what I had with them. The meatballs overpowered everything on the plate. It felt like I sat there for hours working out how to get out of eating them. Whenever I hear posh parents these days ask a five-year-old what they want to eat for dinner, it blows my mind.

The meatballs were covered in thick gravy, which actually helped the process. As long as there was enough gravy, I could disguise not only the taste but the consistency of the clump of mushed-up meat. As time went by, I found ways to avoid eating them. I had a series of methods. Much like Andy Dufresne in *The Shawshank Redemption*, I had to get rid of the evidence. My version of sprinkling the concrete from my escape tunnel in the yard was simply throwing the meatballs out the window when my mum went back into the kitchen for juice. I was five.

I'd sit on the side of the table close to the window. While the guard wasn't looking, I'd throw bits outside. Not enough to raise an alarm, just enough to make it look like I'd enjoyed them.

I also recall once filling my cup with orange juice and dropping bits of meatball in. However, there were too many moving parts with this smuggling method because I had to get it to the kitchen, fish out the meatball pieces, put them in the bin, and pour the orange juice away. All while acting inconspicuous. A five-year-old in a two-bedroom apartment acting inconspicuous does nothing but attract attention.

This continued for a few years. During this time, we moved. Eventually, the meatballs stopped being a regular Sunday thing, but we'd still have them every couple of weeks or so. Each time, I'd work out ways to avoid eating them. When we moved, I made sure to eat by the window.

A few more years passed and we had them less and less often. Eventually, they appeared only a couple of times a year.

Fast-forward to my first year of college. I had moved to London, the year was 2000. I was now living on a diet of ramen cups, microwave meals, and candy bars. Kale wasn't yet a thing, and I wouldn't have cared even if it was. How I'm alive today is beyond me.

I went back home for the Christmas holiday.

My mum asked me what I wanted for dinner. She mentioned meatballs. I vehemently declined.

After a decade and a half, I finally felt it was time to tell my mum that I hated the meatballs.

Replying to my admission with some surprise, she said, "But you used to love them." I told her I never liked them. My mum didn't respond, she just went quiet for a few moments. I could tell there was more to this than I had realized.

When she finally spoke up, she told me she had to make meatballs on Sundays because she couldn't afford anything else. Back then, she had to make the food last. She'd buy mince (or ground beef for those in the United States) early in the week, and we'd have spaghetti Bolognese (which I never had an issue with, obviously), but by Sunday, the rest of the unused meat was made into meatballs. We couldn't afford to waste anything.

I found out that we had them less and less often over the years because my mum was getting on her feet and was able to afford better food. With better jobs came more options. Until the only reason she would still occasionally make them was because she thought I liked them.

Obviously, I felt like an asshole.

Part of me regrets ever bringing it up, but a bigger part of me still hates those goddamn meatballs.

ACID CHICKEN

 Jia Tolentino

THE FIRST ACID CHICKEN WEEKEND WAS JUST BEFORE the 2016 election, a stretch of time I now think about the same way I think about February 2020, a retroactive tinge of naive pleasure suffusing the period just before a seismic shift. Five friends and I had rented a farmhouse in upstate New York, a place with no cell phone service and an extensive record collection and a cedar hot tub in a silent, open field. We drove up on Friday night, with the plan of spending the next day staring at the last fall leaves while tripping on acid. The sun was going to be out, and the house came with a view of the tree-covered mountains, and as we sat down to a big bowl of pesto-slicked linguine that the first car had made for the latecomers, I felt like the richest person in the world.

The free space of an acid trip is best preserved by a small amount of advance planning. You want a space, preferably outdoors, where you can flop around and explore without disturbing (or being disturbed by) sober passersby. You want to be ready for seasonal weather—bug spray in your backpack in the dead of summer, waterproof shoes if it's going to rain. You want music at some point, preferably in a delivery format that doesn't require anyone to look at their phone. Bonus points if someone can bring a visual plaything: a rainbow maker, a cheap disco light. And to me, a food-and-beverage plan is nonnegotiable. Hallucinogens make you lose your appetite: you have to decide to drink water, and the idea of chewing anything other than a sour gummy worm feels appalling. So you've got to have a good late breakfast before tripping, and you want to be able to eat, with an absolute minimum of effort and knife usage—maybe around nine or ten p.m., when you're starting to shudder back toward reality—a warm and friendly meal.

At the farmhouse that morning, as one friend scraped bits of eggs and toast into the trash can and another ceremonially laid out tiny square tabs of LSD on the coffee table, I took a chicken out of the refrigerator, salt-and-peppered it, and stuffed it with lemons and onions and garlic. My friend Frannie roasted a pan of broccoli and a bunch of cherry tomatoes, which went into a big orzo salad with feta and toasted pine nuts, which we assembled in a big ceramic bowl and then covered with foil. The chicken went back into the fridge, and we put the tabs on our tongues.

For the rest of the day, we were in an alien dimension. Dirt shimmered like fairy dust; a small stream on the property became primordial Antarctic meltwater; Frannie, who wasn't tripping but was helping us build fires in the outdoor firepit, kept appearing and disappearing—we decided—like a cartoon elf that had been the subject of regional lore for several hundred years. Everyone's faces looked bewildered and blown open and beautiful. The trees on the mountains swelled like an orchestra, pulsating apricot to scarlet to mauve to indigo. It was a freshly overpowering miracle to be alive on a planet where so many things were growing and dying. It took weeks for the sky to darken, and when it did, we went into the house, opened a bottle of wine, and started playing records. When my stomach suggested to me that we might want to eat in two hours, I turned on the oven and took the chicken out of the fridge.

Raw meat seemed like a lot at the moment, noted one of my friends, who was dancing to Fleetwood Mac like a car-dealership inflatable tube man. But I felt unusually thankful for the chicken, which had once been alive, and for the arbitrary cosmic reality that I was the person cooking the chicken and not the chicken itself. We set the table; when the chicken came out, its skin crackled like the fire. "Acid chicken," someone said. We ate quietly, adjusting to the fact of having bodies. The food gave us a soft reentry back into the world, and an appetite: we reached for seconds and sat at the table for a long time, and in the wee hours, my friend Emma recovered her fine motor skills and made us a melty, cinnamon-dusted apple pie.

Since then I've kept making variations on this simple meal—roasted chicken, a substantial grain salad—on acid-trip days. It works for my friend who doesn't eat red meat; it works for my friend who's vegetarian. It's a meal you want to eat lots of if you haven't consumed anything since breakfast; it smooths over jagged combinations of exhaustion and love. I've made this meal for new parents too, and for friends who are grieving, but over the last four years I've come to think of it as acid chicken. And throughout 2020, I fantasized about it a lot. I was pregnant, so I could not indulge in hallucinogens, and the rest of the acid-chicken scenario felt like science fiction or pornography: a house full of friends, everyone pulling a chair up to the table, talking close without worrying about aerosolized viral droplets, passing a platter, pouring more wine.

Before quarantine, I never thought about the next time I would pull something out of the oven while listening to people laughing. I sometimes picture my last normal social activity of 2020, the first Saturday of March, when a handful of friends came over for improvised Vietnamese lettuce wraps and a viewing of *Ratatouille*. I was sitting on top of my desk with a plate in my lap because there were only four chairs in the apartment and it didn't matter. We were taking care of one another by cooking and eating, by being in the same room. Acid chicken is a quiet reminder of this cyclical constant, this reason to be alive, and the lesson of 2020: the inevitability of weathering much deeper forms of destabilization than the ones you walk into on purpose, and the necessity and the pleasure of giving other people, and ourselves, a soft place to land.

Acid Chicken and Grain Salad

1 roasting chicken
Kosher salt
Black pepper
Paprika
2 lemons
2 onions
1 head of garlic
1 stick (½ cup) unsalted butter

Preheat the oven to 420°F. Dry the chicken off with paper towels, then season it with salt, freshly ground pepper, and paprika. Cut the lemons and onions into quarters, and break the garlic into cloves. Stuff some lemons/onions/garlic in the chicken cavity and scatter the rest around the pan. Melt the butter and pour it on the chicken. Place it in the oven for about an hour, depending on the size of your chicken, and then let it rest for a little bit, basting with the liquid in the pan. Definitely make someone who isn't high carve it.

GRAIN SALAD:

- 2 cups farro
- 1 pound butternut squash
- Olive oil
- Kosher salt
- Black pepper
- 1 bunch of kale
- Garlic
- Walnuts
- Feta
- Lemon juice

This is good for an autumnal trip; if you're doing this in the summer, roast some cherry tomatoes and do lots of herbs in your grain salad instead. But here, cook the farro (usually this involves about a half hour in boiling water, but you can also use chicken broth or apple cider if you want more flavor). While you're doing that, peel and chop the butternut squash, and roast it in a hot oven with olive oil, salt, and pepper. Strip the kale, wash it, dry it, and sauté it in olive oil in a big skillet with some minced garlic, salt, and pepper until it wilts. Chop and toast the walnuts for a couple of minutes; you can do this in the same pan after the kale's done, and put the walnuts to the side. Once the farro's done, drain it, put it in a big bowl, and add the butternut squash, kale, and toasted walnuts. Add the feta and taste for seasoning, adding olive oil and lemon juice as you like.

SUPER CHIEF

 Ted Danson

I GREW UP THREE MILES NORTH OF FLAGSTAFF, ARIZONA. In 1957, my father became the director of a small but well-respected museum and research center, and we were invited to move into a two-story log cabin that belonged to the museum. I was eight years old when we pulled into the driveway for the first time. I looked out of the car window and the first thing I saw was a kid my age duck behind a pine tree. Without thinking, I quietly got out of the car and ducked down behind a couple of boulders. We peeked out of our hiding places at the same time and locked eyes. Game on!

His name was Raymond. Raymond was Hopi. His family lived on the museum property and had a home in a small village on Third Mesa called Bacavi. From that day on, we were inseparable.

Every day was a new adventure. We would set our alarms early so that we would have more time to play, left our homes at dawn with sack lunches, and would only return at dusk. Usually we played some version of "I got you; no, you didn't." Sometimes we jumped on

a couple of horses and rode off bareback in any direction we fancied. We played *Darby's Rangers* for weeks, a war movie we had seen at the Orpheum Theater the week before. Occasionally we would sleep in tents at the foot of the San Francisco peaks. On weekends, we would go to his village on the Hopi mesas and play in and around the kachinas, who were doing ceremonial dances in the same hard-packed dirt plazas they had for centuries.

One evening, Raymond and I were playing chicken, a game where we each had one of his younger brothers on our backs and they would try to pull each other off. I fell and chipped my elbow rather badly. We were hours from the closest hospital, so Raymond's parents took me to the village bonesetter. He set my elbow and within a month it was perfectly healed.

I suppose you could read a couple of books about the Hopi and know more than I knew back then, but my heart and soul knew them completely. I witnessed the Hopi reverence for the land and their respect for all that had come before them. I saw their appreciation of the smallest things. And we laughed. We laughed just for the joy of laughing.

On Sundays, when I returned to Flagstaff and went to the morning service at the Episcopal church with my family, the Hopi dances and the Episcopal church felt somehow very much the same to me.

When I turned thirteen, my parents decided that I would go back east to a private school. I wasn't a very good student and they felt this would be good for my education. I was excited by the idea and ran to tell Raymond. He was quiet for a long time. We spent most of the afternoon whittling in silence. We weren't unhappy with each other, just not sure what this would mean for our friendship.

The rest of that summer passed without us talking about it, and life felt pretty much unchanged. When the day came for me to get on the train back east, I don't think we even said goodbye. We just waved and off I went on my grand adventure.

I took the Santa Fe Super Chief to Chicago, then the 20th Century Limited to Grand Central Station, waited for an hour, and caught a small train to the school. When we arrived, everyone got off the train and walked across a bridge and onto the small campus. The upperclassmen seemed to be in charge of everything, and to a thirteen-year-old, these older boys were quite scary. They seemed to relish the power they had over us. I felt out of place, not sure how to fit in.

After dropping off our bags in our assigned rooms, we all marched off to the dining hall for dinner. The large room was filled with forty or so tables. At one end of each table was a chair for an upperclass boy, with two long benches on either side of the table for the rest of us. There was a pecking order, with the youngest of us at the far end of the table. The food would be delivered to the upperclassman by a preassigned boy, and then passed down the length of the table until it reached us.

I would soon discover that if the meal was something good, like anything with French fries, there would be nothing left by the time it reached the youngest boys. But that first night, the meal was chipped beef in a cream sauce that was poured over a piece of toast, which meant there was a lot of it by the time it got to me. I was just serving myself when the eighteen-year-old at the head of the table yelled down at me, "Hey, kid, pass me the skinned Indian." I didn't understand. He yelled again, "Pass me the skinned Indian!" One of the other kids grabbed the bowl of creamed chipped beef from my hands and sent it back up the table. I wish I could tell you that I jumped up and yelled at that eighteen-year-old, that I had somehow protested. But I didn't. I just sat there. Silent.

When the Christmas holiday came, I took the Super Chief back to Flagstaff. I saw Raymond only once during the three weeks I had off. He was working with his father on their farm near the Hopi mesas. When we did see each other, it was different. I think we both sensed that our lives were taking us in different directions. A week later I got back on the Super Chief and headed east.

Raymond eventually went on to be the vice chair of the Hopi tribe and I became an actor, which is basically a version of "I got you; no, you didn't." We have seen each other maybe a dozen times over the years and it's always the same: lots of stories and easy laughter. But there is a sadness as well.

I was late to the table getting that first taste of bigotry. I think Raymond might have known the cruel phrase already. But on that day, I sat in silence and ate my helping of creamed chipped beef on toast. I have never forgotten the taste of it. It tasted of cowardice. It tasted of innocence lost.

BUTEAU LOVES PASTA, BITCH

 Michelle Buteau

I WISH I COULD REMEMBER THE FIRST TIME I HAD PASTA, BUT I can't. I know I was young, like three- or four-years-old young. While other kids were always going on and on about primary-colored crunchy-ass sugary-sweet cereal that had no taste, I was thinking about pasta all the time.

Maybe my first bite was boxed mac and cheese with that powdered government-ass cheese that I loved so much. OMG. Nothing says childhood and/or hangovers like that powdered cheese! It's like a delicious science experiment. Those packets got me feeling like Matt Damon in *The Martian*, just ready to fuck up something delicious! Oh lawd, and when Velveeta came out with the creamy packet? Back. The. Fuck. Up!

Or maybe my first bite was spaghetti Bolognese? Talk about a damn delicious way to sneak in the vegetables. That slow-simmer tomato yummy good-good is everything. Even to this day, it's one of my favorite meals, and anytime I eat it, I have to put on an old T-shirt because it's about to get messed up and stained up! The fun, delicate swirl you make with spaghetti on your fork, and, if you're lucky enough, know how to do it in a spoon? OMG. What in the *Stanley Tucci: Searching for Italy* is going on? The moment you're finally able to swirl that perfect bite of Bolognese good-good from fork to spoon and fork to mouth, you'll feel like you're that subway performer who's mastered playing the drums and harmonica at the same time. Who's ready for *America's Got Talent* though? (Ha! No shade. And now that I think about it, they're not reading this.)

Or, honestly, my first pasta could've been from the Chinese restaurant in my Jersey neighborhood growing up. My parents and I would go every Friday night and order the same thing:

Shrimp fried rice

Spare ribs

Chicken and broccoli

Chicken lo mein

Don't forget to eat your fortune cookie for good luck!

Sounds basic now, but as a young kid growing up in Jersey, that was a night out, honey!

I could never get enough lo mein. I was obsessed with the savory flavors. At the time, I could never pinpoint what they were, but now I know that hoisin sauce, sesame oil, and "soy-a-sauce" (lol sorry not sorry) are a magical trio to coat that not-quite-spaghetti-but-still-fun-to-slurp pasta. Shout-out to another amazing vehicle for getting kids to eat vegetables. Savory veggies and pasta. Whoever came up with this shit, you're the real MVP.

Ya see, it's impossible for me to narrow down one thing and one recipe when *my* one thing is pasta. Noodles. Spaghetti. Macaroni. Whatever you call it, it's unfeasible to pick one top pasta dish. It's like picking your favorite child or favorite Whitney Houston song, ya just can't do it. And if you can, you're an asshole. Rigatoni, shells, vermicelli, pad thai, drunken noodles, penne?!? They all have wonderfully different textures and pair with such different tastes, but the common denominator—DE PASTA, BITCH. I'm sorry, James Kennedy from *Vanderpump Rules*—in this case, it *is about the pasta*. It's my Terry Lewis and Jimmy Jam (lolz old references).

No merci, hunty, I don't need your artisanal bread. I could give a shit about the brick oven that you built yourself. But if you come to me with a lasagna with béchamel? Panties are dropping and you're still in the running to become *America's Next Top Model*, bish!

I love tomato sauce, sauce, gravy, whatever you wanna call it, so damn much it doesn't have to be homemade. Gimme a hard-to-open jar to spank any ol' time. I love noodles so damn much I don't care if it's expensive or cheap as fuck. Cup O' Noodles soup? I'm sorry, did you say there are technically no active ingredients in the cup but just add water and poof! You've got soup with noodles? Yes, okay—where do I sign up? If I'm sick and you'd like to get me chicken soup for my soul, aww that's so nice—but it better have noodles up in there 'cause then what's the point? I don't need a fancy, overpriced, what-in-the-eighteen-dollars bag of hipster rigatoni either, because it's just a flour, eggs, and water bag of pasta. I'll happily and nappily take that last box of the broken spaghetti from the bodega and hit her up with some salt, pepper, butter, and lemon. As long as I get to boil that delicious good-good carb load in hot water, a pinch of salt, and a dollop of olive oil, *yas*. Zero fucks given!

One of my uncles is the archbishop of Jamaica (I know, take several seats to wrap that around ya mind! Ha!) and growing up we'd have a lot of nuns who would visit from Jamaica. One day, when I was about eight or nine years old, I got home from school, and Sister Joseph and her nun friends were hungry and didn't know where to go and what to do. So I whipped up my easy peasy, buttery breezy noodles for them. This was decades ago *and they still talk about it*.

"Whut th'ird gradah maken' dem noooodles like dat, ah wha dat!?"

And ya know what? I still make dem nooooodles like dat every day for lunch for my toddling twins. I make *all* the pasta dishes for them and sneak in *all* the vegetables. And they love it.

When my husband and I were trying to conceive, it was pretty rough. We tried for five whole years before deciding to go down the surrogacy route. It was painstaking, expensive, and just a wild time. I wasn't sure how it was going to go. Being pregnant is the first part of the process to parenthood, so if I was working with a surrogate, would I be involved at all?

But then I had a phone call with my surrogate in the early stages of our pregnancy. I asked her if she had any cravings. She said she hated spaghetti with meatballs but it was all she was craving.

I cried because I knew immediately this was my child and all would be okay.

Easy Peasy,
Buttery Breezy Noodles

INGREDIENTS

Olive oil
Salt
As much pasta as you want
Salted butter
Black pepper
Garlic powder

Bring water to a boil, add a dollop of olive oil and a pinch of salt.

Throw in that pasta like you're mad at it and stir. Bring down to a teeny-tiny bubble.

Drain the pasta when it's cooked but do not rinse it in water! Who raised you?!?

Throw it back in the pot, place it on low heat, add a dollop of butter, a crack of black pepper, and a skosh of garlic powder.

Ya done, bitch!

A WARM HOLIDAY MEMORY FROZEN IN TIME

 Mark D. Sylvester

M Y ELDERLY MOTHER PEACEFULLY PASSED AWAY THIS morning, July 5, 2021. An event like this causes you to reflect on childhood memories. Most people probably have an avalanche of memories to ponder, but I don't.

I knew from a very young age that I was different and gay. As many parents did in the 1970s, mine sought treatment to cure my homosexuality. The barbaric treatments of the time left most of my early childhood memories cold. However, this morning I recalled, for the first time in years, the joy that Christmas cookies brought to my mom every holiday. I thought about how consistent they were in an otherwise inconsistent childhood. They always tasted the same every year, just like a Big Mac tastes no matter where or when you buy one.

My favorite was her simple honey pecan cookies. She would always make several dozen and freeze them. They are amazing about two minutes out of the freezer.

I always wondered if she realized she could keep fitting more cookies in the freezer as December progressed because it was my holiday cookie box. As I aged, I came to understand that while my mom never understood me, she did love me.

This memory is a warm one.

Honey Pecan Cookies

1 cup sugar
½ cup salted butter, softened
2 large eggs
2 tablespoons honey
1 teaspoon vanilla
1½ cups flour
2 teaspoons baking powder
¼ teaspoon salt
Pecan halves

Preheat the oven to 350°F.

Whip the sugar and butter until light and fluffy. Beat in the eggs, one at a time. Add the honey and vanilla. In another bowl, mix the flour, baking powder, and salt. Fold the wet ingredients into the flour mixture, and drop by small teaspoonfuls onto a greased cookie sheet at least 2 inches apart. Place half a pecan on top of each cookie. Bake for about 12 to 14 minutes.

Tip: For people with nut allergies, you can substitute half a candied cherry.

CHAINS

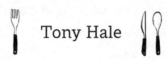

Tony Hale

I'M A PROUD LOVER OF CHAIN RESTAURANTS. WHEN PEOPLE disparage them, I'm offended. When trying to find a place to eat and someone says, "I only see chains" . . . great. What's the problem?

Have you ever compared a chain dessert with the local farm-to-table dessert? The chain's brownie sundae *demolishes* the hipster's mini tart with a "dollop" of flavored foam. It's quantity over quality. And I'm all in. When it's time to medicate some feelings, quantity rules the roost.

I love cruises. Not for the adventure but because they're pretty much a Cheesecake Factory on water. Heaven.

I'm sure this is rooted in wanting certainty in life and expectations matched every time. It's comforting. A basic marinara, simple fried cheese, and the faithful brownie. If you're judging me, I get it. But come back to me after you've had a hot chocolate chip cookie served in a skillet from BJ's with the ice cream of your choice on top, or Red Lobster's Cheddar Bay Biscuits. Disagree with me then.

RECIPE...

1. Choose a restaurant that has no fewer than five hundred locations.

2. Open menu/catalog.

3. Feast.

4. Continue feast by choosing whichever dessert ends with the word *paradise*, *decadence*, *madness*, or *explosion*.

5. Remove shame from this entire equation.

SOLITARY PIZZA

 Mari Andrew

"NO FOOD IS SADDER THAN A PERSONAL PIZZA" IS A text I once read and promptly disagreed with.

There are hundreds of objectively sadder foods:

An unsold pie in a deli case, a celebratory food to be shared at a bustling table now wasting away in isolation.

And, for that matter, a never-to-be-consumed cake in the grocery store bakery with a hopeful pink scribble reading "Happy Birthday!" (The exclamation point makes it a good ten times sadder.)

Or even sadder, a birthday cake for a party where nobody shows up. But perhaps worse, a birthday cake for a party where people show up *but* everyone is on a diet and no one eats the cake. These cake scenarios might be equal in sadness.

There is the sadness of an unattended lemonade stand or the sadness of free samples when no one takes any. An untouched tray full of mini quiches offered by a cheerful employee beckoning "Would you like to try some quiche today?" to uninterested shoppers is so much sadder than a personal pizza.

Few beverages are sadder than poorly made complimentary hot chocolate, consumed by exactly one person who needs a little cheering up, who very well might spill it down her coat.

There are sad foods from personal memories: the sadness of the frozen dinner my newly divorced dad heated up in the dirty microwave in his sloppy transitional apartment that he shared with a roommate.

There's the sadness of the store-bought cookies I brought to school that nobody ate, because Missy Russo's birthday was the same day and she was more popular and thus her (stay-at-home mom's homemade) cupcakes were preferred.

There's the sadness of the Looney Tunes fruit snacks I brought in my lunch and decided were too babyish to eat in public, so I discarded them in the brown paper bag with my name on it and pined for them later.

When a date got up and left *in the middle of our dinner*, throwing down insufficient cash with an insufficient "I'm not feeling this—take care," my plate of pasta was extremely sad; it only became sadder when the waitress asked me if I wanted it packaged up to go. I did.

There's the stunningly sad image burned in my memory of an old man eating a bad-quality blueberry muffin alone outside a museum café, his belt tragically crooked and his hand shaking as he struggled with the wrapper.

There's the sadness of the chocolate my mom bought me as a treat to comfort myself when she was away on business. There's the sadness of the chocolates I ate from the gift shop as dessert after a tray of extremely sad hospital food. It's rarely mentioned, but chocolate can be really sad.

You see, Sad Food is not the same as Solitude Food. And a personal pizza is a Solitude Food—therefore not very sad. I buy a personal pizza when I'm anticipating a glorious night entirely to myself: feet up on the coffee table, sparkling water I drink straight from the bottle, some indulgent totally uncool wine (like a merlot from the Dave Matthews winery), and a show I've seen a hundred times or a delectable YouTube deep dive. Just me, melted cheese, and the Thanksgiving episode of *Gilmore Girls* or a Kardashian makeup tutorial. That's divine solitude.

Solitude Food is often found on room-service menus, when you're spread out on the oversize bed of a chain hotel and contemplating whether to send for the burger or the salmon on your company's credit card as you flip through cable channels and settle on an eighties movie.

I love the Solitude Food of bar snacks while traveling alone, when you decide to forgo a proper dinner in lieu of tapas or roasted peanuts or a basket of bread.

Airplane food in all its bizarre temperatures (chilled dinner roll, warm granola bar) is good Solitude Food, especially when accompanied by a sitcom binge among the clouds.

A coffee shop offers a wealth of Solitude Food: a croissant balancing at the edge of a table, making room for a book and an oversize coffee saucer, especially if that pastry has been ordered as "the usual."

And there are few Solitude Foods better than a bucket of popcorn to oneself in the back of a movie theater on a rainy weekday afternoon of playing hooky.

But, as we've all experienced, Solitude Food can *become* a Lonely Food—and that's where it becomes sad. Solitude is slippery and can morph into loneliness with an accidental listen to a particularly evocative song on your shuffle, or when the scene isn't as charming as you anticipated, or when something goes awry in your pursuit of Solitude Food and it sinks into something very lonely.

I'm thinking of times when I thought it would be cozy to spend a holiday alone, only to end up looking at an unlit phone over and over while eating an overly festive casserole.

I'm thinking of a fellow barista at the coffee shop where I used to work, an enthusiastic home cook named Sarah who told me of her harrowing attempt to splurge on a magnificent pasta feast for herself after work one day. Anticipating a delightful cooking adventure to soothe a recent heartbreak, she braved Whole Foods at evening rush hour, and a concatenation of disasters ensued: Sarah spilled pine nuts all over the bulk aisle to the horror of a grumpy employee; she ordered the wrong meat and felt too sheepish to replace it; her credit card didn't work at checkout and a manager had to get involved so she could write a check for her bounty. "So, how many people are you cooking for tonight?" the cashier asked to diffuse her agony as a long line of impatient people behind her glared. "Oh, just one," she responded, and her Solitude Food instantly turned into Lonely Food.

I'm thinking of the rare moments when I've felt lonely while traveling solo, like after I took myself out for a celebratory dinner following a big speech in Athens and was ushered to a back table to make room for the couples and showcase the groups of friends in the front.

Mid-spanakopita, I looked around and realized that nobody at the restaurant could possibly infer why I ordered a coupe of champagne, nor would they care to. I sipped it unceremoniously, wishing I knew anybody in this whole city who could toast with me. A solo glass of bubbly to fete an accomplishment is a hopelessly sad beverage.

Living alone in New York provides a nonstop emotional dance between the splendor of solitude and the affliction of loneliness, which alternate during any given subway ride or studio apartment dinner. I suppose it has to do with the New York dance of feeling extremely significant or extremely insignificant, depending on weather, mood, recent interaction with a stranger, or how capable I feel of carrying my groceries up the stairs alone. I can feel significantly solitary or pathetically lonely in the span of an hour, and therefore my meals also bounce capriciously between the two states.

Take this lemon risotto, which I've made a million times since I moved to New York. When I made it the first time, it was Sad Food: two dinner plans fell through and cooking risotto alone in my studio gave me that distinct feeling that everyone else in the city was out, in love, and throwing their heads back in laughter with fashionable and adoring friends. I ended up making too much of the recipe, and the excess enhanced my melancholy: no one to share with. A personal pizza could have been sadder, I suppose, but not by much. I lapped it up while unsuccessfully attempting to soothe myself with nonsense, but no reality TV would fill the emptiness in my spirit. I went to bed early, risotto rice splashed on my walls.

Now that I've mastered the portions, it's my go-to Solitude Food: for an evening when the only company I crave is a podcast and my oven light. It's for an evening after a long day when I'm buzzing from interacting and I crave a few hours of complete neutrality in utter aloneness, the type of evening when I set down my bags on the floor and my apartment feels like a whole kingdom devoted to my desires. Everything on my walls is exactly at my eye level, the couch has molded to my shape, my cat knows only my voice, and my kitchen is arranged as I would have it. The queen has returned; now the party begins. I take out my white wine and my rice and my Parmesan, and I create a royal banquet for one.

If I make lemon risotto *too* often, it's in danger of becoming a Sad Food once again—just as a personal pizza Monday through Friday would be a tragedy, not an indulgence. Solo risotto every night of the week, as luxurious as it sounds, would be indicative of a lonesome rut, not treasured alone time.

So I make it when I'm consciously forgoing plans in pursuit of a stupendous evening in slippers. There's nothing sad about a meal all to oneself if it's being enjoyed.

Lemony Kale Risotto

Adapted from Klancy Miller's *Cooking Solo*

Add more kale if you're feeling virtuous; pair with Albariño if you're feeling cheeky. Grate some extra cheese, always.

MAKES 4 SERVINGS

YOU'LL NEED:

- Olive oil
- 1 Spanish onion, diced
- 1 cup Arborio or sushi rice
- 2 cups chicken or vegetable stock
- 1 cup white wine
- ½ cup plus a small handful freshly grated Parmesan cheese
- Sprinkle of sea salt
- Freshly ground black pepper
- 1 bunch of dinosaur kale, stems and ribs removed, thinly sliced
- Grated zest of 1 lemon

In a large saucepan, heat a healthy drizzle of olive oil over medium heat. Add the onion and cook, stirring occasionally, until translucent, about 5 minutes. Add the rice, stir to coat it with olive oil, and cook, stirring frequently to prevent sticking, until the grains are slightly translucent, about 4 minutes.

Stir in 1 cup of the stock and bring the mixture to a boil over high heat. Add the wine and adjust the heat to maintain a simmer. Cook, stirring frequently, until the rice absorbs all the liquid. Add the remaining 1 cup stock and cook, still stirring, until the rice becomes tender and creamy, 25 to 30 minutes total.

Stir in ½ cup of the Parmesan, salt, and a few grinds of pepper. Taste and add more salt if necessary. Simmer for 5 more minutes.

While the risotto finishes, heat a couple of tablespoons of olive oil in a large cast-iron skillet over medium-high heat, tilting the pan to coat the bottom. Add the kale and a pinch of salt and cook, stirring occasionally, until wilted and bright green, 2 to 3 minutes.

Sprinkle one-quarter of the remaining handful of Parmesan cheese over each portion and add a little lemon zest on top. Arrange the kale over the risotto. Serve hot.

PEST-O CHANGE-O

 Sloane Crosley

I WANTED TO SET MY KITCHEN ON FIRE. IN THIS, I WAS NOT alone. Presumably, other people did not have it out for my *specific* kitchen, but in March 2020, all of New York City was forced to tap into their inner gourmand. Some embraced the challenge, baking what was left of their sanity into sourdough bread. But my inner gourmand was so buried, I'd have had better luck extracting my own bone marrow. Like many New Yorkers who'd always fancied themselves culturally curious, it turned out my primary prepandemic hobby was simply eating food in public. And so, during those anxious nights when it didn't make logistical or emotional sense for me to broil a whole branzino or beat egg whites for a party of one, there was only one dish that made me feel just a little bit better. Though *dish* is a big word for it.

Have you ever heard of pasta? It's great, you'll love it.

Because dumping red sauce into a saucepan somehow invited even more depressing associations than an elaborate dinner for one (see: Macaulay Culkin in *Home Alone*, a dish of mac and cheese and a goblet of milk before him, or Jennifer Lopez in *The Wedding Planner*, dining on her sofa), I'd been avoiding pasta altogether. But then one day, as I was scrolling through Instagram, I saw what looked like an uncharacteristically unappetizing pile of green slop on Fanny Singer's grid. I vaguely know Fanny. She is the daughter of Alice Waters of Chez Panisse fame. She grew up in the house responsible for the farm-to-table movement. For the most part, I tended to shelve Fanny's vibrant photos of farmers market hauls (Calamansi limes! Panache figs! Cardamom cake! Pretty word + foodstuff!) in the same category that I shelved aspirational fashion. *Sure, maybe one day. Maybe in another life.* It's not that one can't decently mimic California's bounty in New York (we are not lacking in farmers markets, butchers, or bakeries), but, to me at least, it often feels practically prohibitive or expensive or both. It's too much cilantro left to wilt in the crisper. And with COVID regulations? A farmers market meant an awfully long wait to peruse radishes.

But when I saw that bowl of green mush (dip? was it perhaps dip? mortar for the Grinch's house?) on Fanny's page, it called to me. It looked doable, whatever it was. I'd been consuming a disturbing amount of beige and packaged foods and, stuck in the stale air of my apartment, I wanted to ingest something fresh. I wanted to eat the same things they were eating in Northern California, where the yards were more spacious and the sirens less audible, where you could walk outside without touching a doorknob all your neighbors had just touched. That sounded nice. But not so nice that I was about to make a complicated terrine of anything.

So I wrote to Fanny, who explained that I was looking at kale and parsley pesto. I had never made pesto before and thus did not have even a baseline understanding of what was involved (only that it was off-limits to those with tree-nut allergies). I was surprised by how simple she made it sound, how accessible. Her instructions were purposefully imprecise, coming from someone who finds fluency and joy in cooking. "A fistful of pine nuts." "A couple of glugs of olive oil." And the best part? "It freezes well." There was only one warning issued: do *not* add more kale than basil, or I'd "live to regret it." Having now made The Pesto more than a dozen times, I can tell you this is as ironclad a rule as *Gremlins'* "Don't feed them after midnight."

The Pesto is delicious, sure. Consider the source. You can spread it on toast, put it in pasta, mix it in scrambled eggs, or cover your walls with it and lick it off. But for me, it began to please more than my palate. The ritual of making it became important; throwing all the ingredients into a Cuisinart food processor and watching them spin is the savory version of cake icing. It's colorful and gratifying to watch something become more delicious than the sum of its parts. Adding more ingredients to taste reminded me of being a kid, of making "potions" in the kitchen (in a mock cauldron of my mother's Tupperware). There was also something comforting about knowing that during such a messed-up time, The Pesto was something I couldn't really mess up. It was mentally healthy to get comfortable with this one microscopic certainty. I got so into it, I developed a system whereby I'd consume one fresh serving of The Pesto and scrape the rest into an ice cube tray, popping out a portion for one whenever I wanted it (stressful days were two-cube kinda days). This did not feel sad or lonely, it felt ingenious.

It also served as a launching pad to help me get more creative in the kitchen, replacing the kale with chard or collard greens, sautéing shallots, broccolini, cherry tomatoes, shrimp, and leeks that I mixed in with my leaf-flecked fusilli.

Did The Pesto save me? Did it keep me sane during quarantine? No, of course not. If my sanity could be solved by pasta sauce, I wouldn't need to worry about it in the first place. But it did provide me with a dinner that I looked forward to. Dinner was a way to demarcate the days, and the days were in some desperate need of demarcating. The Pesto is the only dish from that time period that I still make. Now that I want to burn down my kitchen only *once* a week, I've had people over to my apartment. I've made them dinner, whipping up The Pesto on autopilot while we chat. Like a person who actually enjoys cooking, now I get to share a dish with others that I learned to make when I was alone. Only the basil and I know what it was like back then, when it was just the two of us. The Pesto always gets compliments. To which I say: Oh, this? It's nothing, really.

Fanny's Pandemic Kale Pesto

INGREDIENTS

Pepitas or pine nuts—toast in an oven or cast-iron pan until lightly browned. (Hemp seeds, walnuts, pistachios, or almonds will also work well.) Approximately ¼ cup nuts per bunch of kale.

Garlic—2 peeled cloves per bunch of kale

Parmesan cheese—grate on medium, using approximately ½ cup per bunch of kale.

Fine sea salt, freshly ground black pepper, and a pinch of hot chili flakes—essential seasoning!

A bunch or 3 of fresh basil leaves (or any brassica if basil is scarce)

A bunch or 2 of fresh kale of any variety (lacinato, curly, etc.)—you'll just use the leaves: strip them from any thick or woody stems. If you're using baby kale, skip this step. Save any especially tough stems for uses like in soup or veggie broth.

Parsley—the plucked leaves from a bunch

Juice and zest of 1 lemon (finely zested)

Extra-virgin olive oil—find a good mild, verdant one and use as much as you need to lubricate and loosen the sauce without it getting too greasy.

METHOD

First, pulse the solid ingredients: add the pepitas or pine nuts and garlic to the bowl of a food processor or a large bowl with an immersion blender, and pulse to grind.

Add the grated cheese, salt, pepper, and hot chili flakes, and pulse again.

Next, add the basil, raw kale leaves, parsley leaves, and the lemon juice and zest. Process until all the ingredients are well combined.

Add the olive oil. With the blade running, pour the oil into the mixture. Process until the oil is incorporated.

Season to taste: Try a spoonful and add more salt, pepper, lemon juice, and/or cheese as desired. If the kale pesto tastes especially bitter, add ¼ teaspoon maple syrup or honey to balance it. If fresh basil is available, sub in basil for one-quarter of the kale for a more classic flavor profile.

Freezes well!

RAS MALAI

Tulica Singh

O
F ALL THE INDIAN SWEETS, RAS MALAI WAS HER FAVOR-
ite. She couldn't remember why.

STEP 1: Make the sauce (rabri)

Heat 3 cups of milk on a warm, medium flame.

He called her his gift because she was born on his birthday. Perhaps it would seem more fated if he didn't intentionally schedule the
C-section for that day. But it was undoubtedly sweeter that he would
choose to share it with her.

And as fate or scheduling would have it, she turned out to be a car-
bon copy of her father. The second daughter of four, and his proclaimed
favorite. Don't worry, the other sisters were fine with it. As an Indian
dad, he was by nature emotionally unavailable and prone to unpredictable outbursts. But as his mini me, she felt a sort of unspoken loyalty.
Everyone loved their mother. He needed someone too.

STEP 2: Add the sweetness

When the milk begins to boil, add saffron and sugar, carefully stirring every 2 to 3 minutes.

In those first few years, she was the apple of his eye. He rented a video camera, with money he didn't have, to document every second with his little gift.

The more she grew, the more parts of him she would share, and she cherished every single one of them. He could whistle through his teeth, so she learned to whistle through hers. He wore only pants, so she demanded only pants. And when her parents fought so intensely they talked of divorce, he found her waiting in his car, ready to *Paper Moon* it, just the two of them.

STEP 3: Make the chenna (paneer balls)

In a separate bowl, bring 5 cups of milk to a boil and add lemon to make it curdle. Rinse the curdled milk and wrap it tightly and securely in cheesecloth.

She also shared some of his worst traits. Uncontrollable body hair, heartburn, anxiety, and depression. But, of course, as an Indian man he would never admit to the last two. So he hid them with a fiery temper.

And as fate or scheduling would have it, she got older and therefore more susceptible to his bouts of anger. Especially when she committed the worst offense a daughter could in this dangerous world of kidnappers and rapists. She got her period. An eleven-year-old with a woman's body became the target of strange men's unwanted attention. He could not control the men, but he could control her. So he used the Indian weapon of choice: shame.

Overnight she was no longer young, she was naive. Her clothes were an invitation to get attacked. And her lack of constant vigilance would result in her imminent kidnapping.

Any conversation they had was an opportunity to unload his paranoia.

HER: I'll take the chicken to go.
HIM: No, leave it, they'll poison it.

HER: Bye, Papa, I'm going to school.
HIM: Did you check under the car? Men wait with knives to slice your Achilles tendon so they can more easily kidnap you and sell you into human trafficking.

HER: What's Aji's address again?
HIM: Don't trust anyone.

STEP 4: Knead the chenna

Once all the liquid is squeezed from the chenna, knead it until it's smooth. Then separate it into pieces and flatten them into smaller discs.

Though he might have changed, she still wanted to be his favorite. So she hid herself as much as she could. Doubling sports bras and donning big T-shirts to hide any sign of being a human female. She agreed with whatever he said and learned when to talk and when to shut up. She created the perfect persona of the perfect daughter.

It wasn't until she left her childhood home that she learned she had become numb. A shell of a person sleepwalking through life. At home she was so good at hiding, she forgot who she was. But when she was away, she had no one to hide from and was free to feel again.

She began to trust strangers. Hug them, confront them, and even say "I love you." She wasn't ready to share this version of herself with him, so she made the compromise most daughters of immigrants make: militant code-switching.

She lived her life in two worlds. But one was easier than the other. Slowly she found herself growing further and further away from the man who could whistle through his teeth like she could. Their conversations became just a nod and a smile from her as he spoke of the growing dangers of the world.

This all seemed normal. Parents are crazy, right?

STEP 5: Submerge into syrup

Bring water, sugar, and cardamom to a boil, and bathe the discs in the warm sugary liquid.

It wasn't until her friends became fathers themselves that she realized something was wrong. They asked their daughters how their day was. They cared, they listened. And not once did they talk about slashing Achilles tendons. . . . What the hell? She had no idea this was an option!

She decided that not only did she want this type of relationship with her father, she deserved it! She broke her monosyllabic phone-call rule and surprised him with an impromptu conversation. She asked how his day was, and to her surprise he answered honestly. They had an extremely pleasant conversation. Everything she had been dreaming of.

STEP 6: Remove from syrup

Take the chenna out of their sweet, safe home and squeeze any excess sugar out of them.

But the dream was dashed when his omnipresent TV broke the news of riots at a Trump rally. It was 2016 and the chasm between conservatives and their liberal children was growing more and more dire. (Although he was an immigrant, her father lived in Fox News territory and became a staunch Trump supporter.) Angry at the "rioters," he began to regurgitate some MAGA propaganda. And she, now an adult with opinions, responded with her leftist ideas.

In one second she went from favorite daughter to liberal enemy.

He laid into her with a surprising amount of fear-filled vitriol. She was once again naive, shallow, and inviting danger. The dream had so quickly turned into a nightmare. She hated every second and wanted so desperately to return to a pleasant conversation, so she yelled: "I don't want to talk about this anymore!"

But what he heard was: *I don't want to talk to you anymore.*

So he granted her wish and told her they never had to speak again. The line went dead, and then her heart stopped.

She had never been disowned before, so she went to the expert: her older sister who shared her father's proclivity for red-faced political arguments, who'd collected three or four disownments in her time. Her sister explained that their mother was traveling, so he needed to get his anger out somehow. "Don't worry, it will blow over."

They hung up and, like clockwork, her father sent what she assumed was an apology in the form of a text with a string of emojis. But now that she had seen what a father could be, this wouldn't suffice. He chose a politician over his favorite daughter. She wasn't his favorite anymore.

After that she distanced herself even further, speaking of him only to therapists and on third dates. And with the distance, the memories grew more and more painful:

- Leaving her alone in the hospital waiting room as an infant
- Calling her weak and spoiled for crying if he was "mean" to her
- Telling her she was a stupid fucking idiot when she got lost snowshoeing and didn't take her phone

Away from the casual cruelty of her beloved father, she began to identify these memories as wounds. And with a great deal of work, she began to heal them by choosing the millennial indulgence of self-care over giving in to familial obligations. In time she settled into a person she liked.

And then one day she got a phone call. Maui, her family's dog, was sick.

STEP 7: Cool down

Combine the chenna with the rabri and bring to the fridge to chill together.

Maui was a beautiful golden retriever, albeit not the smartest or most graceful. Like most dads, her father never wanted a dog. So he called her the "dumb blond bitch." To him, Maui was a clumsy shit machine that stole food and destroyed furniture. He didn't show her the most affection, but somehow she always listened to him.

Maui was young and virile, but lung cancer moved quickly. She deteriorated with frightening speed.

The daughters rushed home to be with her. They watched in horror as Maui spent weeks gasping for air, caught in a never-ending asthma attack. When the suffering outweighed the living, they finally decided to take her to the vet and have her put to sleep. Everyone jumped into the car except for the patriarch. He opted to go to Walmart instead, an astonishingly callous choice, but they had learned not to expect much from him.

Maui took her last breath in the parking lot at the vet's office, surrounded by the tear-filled faces of the women who loved her.

When they arrived home, briny and broken, their father greeted them with cheap plastic bags filled with cheap plastic products. Flashlights, first-aid kits, slippers with grips on the bottom. A cornucopia of safety items nobody wanted.

He desperately sought affirmation that he'd done a good thing. But they ignored him. All except for his favorite daughter.

In this moment she saw the man she used to share so much with. He wanted to protect them at all costs because he had failed to protect the dog he secretly loved. The dog that listened to him because they shared many quiet moments when no one was looking. The dog he gave salami to every night. The dog he didn't have the strength to say goodbye to.

And when she saw this man, she also saw the memories she had forgotten:

- The time he cried when she went to her first homecoming
- The time he defended her to the cops when she threw an insane rager
- The time he took responsibility for not making her feel safe enough to come out of the closet

She wanted to hug him, to tell him it was okay. But they didn't do that. So she let the status quo overshadow them both.

STEP 8: Add pistachios

Once cooled, sprinkle with sliced pistachios and serve!

That night, she went upstairs for a midnight snack. When she got to the kitchen, he was already there, making his nightly popcorn. Midnight snacking was another thing they shared.

They said a stilted hello and he turned back to the microwave, diligently watching the kernels pop.

She went to the fridge and that's where she saw it, the box of ras malai. She hadn't had it in forever. This was a special box from a fancy Indian restaurant, not the usual factory box. The spongy milk balls were pristine and topped with green. She always forgot about the pistachios.

A final memory rushed back to her. She was four years old and sitting safely in her dad's lap, repeating the only Hindi she could remember: "Cheez dedo!"

For everyone else, this would translate to "Give me the things!" but for them, "cheez" was their shared word for pistachios. He would peel them, she would eat them. That was their deal.

She quietly plated the dessert, one for her and one for him. He looked down at the small gift from his daughter and smiled.

"Ras malai, my favorite."

THE FRANKOPHILE

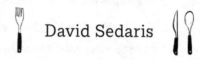

David Sedaris

"YOU EAT LIKE A CHILD," MY SISTER AMY SAID TO ME NOT too terribly long ago when I had a thirty-three-inch waist.

That sounded like an insult so of course I put up a fight. "And you're a whore."

"I mean it," she said. "Look at you, making Jell-O. And what did you have for lunch? Hot dogs!"

This was true, but in my defense they were Wagyu beef hot dogs, hand forged by artisans. Yes, there were most likely lips in them, and eyelids, but the price—nineteen dollars a pack—along with the fact that they were certified "organic," meant, most likely, that the cow had been killed before her face was peeled off.

I'm not a snob when it comes to hot dogs, far from it. I used to love the ones I bought on the street when I first lived in New York back in the early nineties. Pair one with a bag of plain potato chips and there was nothing better. I usually ate while perched on a low wall of some sort. If there was nothing around that fit that description, I'd impale myself on a fire hydrant. Traffic would pass, spewing exhaust, and that added to the overall experience, making it, in my mind, cosmopolitan. When I look back at myself—that massive, five-sided opening nut halfway up my anus—I see a kid, though I was in my early thirties at the time.

The dozen or so hot dogs I've eaten on the street since returning to New York almost thirty years later have all been disconcertingly limp and mushy. I think they languished in their steaming baths for too long. There was no give to them, and so I started cooking my own at home. Most often they're the fancy, handcrafted kind. And they're delicious.

In Chicago, where I spent my late twenties, they'd put anything on a hot dog: cucumber, tomatoes, molten cheese—gravy wouldn't surprise me, or candied walnuts—but I like mine with just mustard and a slaw I get my boyfriend, Hugh, to make. He used to pull out a bun and join me until Amy got in his ear. Now, like her, he won't have anything to do with hot dogs, not even the nineteen-dollar ones. Not even on special occasions like Frankfurter Fridays.

"Since when is that a thing?" he asked when I first introduced it.

THE FRANKOPHILE

Hugh eats sweetbreads, which are thyroid glands. He's had brains and intestines and tails, so I really don't see what his problem is.

"It's the mixing it together part I don't believe in," he says.

Normally we have some sort of a salad for lunch. That's not a complaint. I'm very fortunate when it comes to food. I don't know anyone who eats better than I do. Hugh does the cooking and is happy to spend three hours putting dinner together. There are never any shortcuts with him. He makes his own piecrusts and mayonnaise—his own pasta if there's time. If it were possible to lay his own eggs or at least sit on them until they hatch, I have no doubt that he'd do it.

We eat dinner at the table, always by candlelight—no TV, no phones. Two or three times a week we have company, and they always say, usually between the first and the second courses, "Oh my God. David, you are so lucky to have Hugh."

I don't think anyone's ever reversed that and told him how lucky he is to have me. They see him in the kitchen stitching up a leg of lamb or flambéing something. They see him mixing drinks and setting the table. What I do is more in the background. It's stuff people can't see, like buying glue or making Jell-O.

"I'd hardly call that making," Amy said the day she told me that I ate like a child. True, it's not terribly difficult to open a box or boil water, but then there's the stirring part and that should count for something. I like mixing mine almost but not quite enough, so that there's a chewy skin on the bottom.

"Disgusting!" Amy says, but it's like fruit leather, only cold and quivering, and as close to actual fruit as a can of Hawaiian Breeze air freshener is to an actual Hawaiian breeze. Jell-O, like Gatorade, tastes like a color rather than a flavor.

The lemon, for instance, doesn't smack of actual lemon, but only of yellow. The lime tastes green and the strawberry red. There's a new kind—the box reads *peach* for some reason—and it tastes beige.

Where, I wonder, are the Jell-O artisans? Why not make mint flavor? Grapefruit? Carrot might actually be nice, or NyQuil. I used to mix one red with another when I was young and pour it into the mold my mother used for Bundt cakes. Into the frigid hole in the center I would cram green grapes, maybe topped with Cool Whip. After childhood I somehow forgot all about Jell-O. It was in the attic of my food memory, alongside Tang and soft pouches of Carnation Instant Breakfast, until the second year of the pandemic. What brought it back to me was a diet. I'd been on it for a week or two and had just reached the point where I was wandering the grocery store, looking for something, anything, that wasn't fattening. *How many calories are in Saran Wrap*, I remember wondering. Then I turned a corner and there it was.

When I was young, Jell-O was all just horse hooves and sugar. Now they make a new kind that's horse hooves and *artificial* sugar. It has just eight calories per serving, which is nothing—a single potato chip has more than eight calories.

I'm not sure exactly how much weight I put on during the pandemic—scales mesh too neatly with my particular mental illness—but I knew that my shirts and jackets no longer fit. I normally gain in my chest, and in my back, of all places. I've never followed an established diet; rather, I tend to make them up. My last one involved walking twenty miles a day and eating a lot of popcorn from a bag. For my latest, I walk fifteen miles a day, eat half as much as I normally would, and fill up on Jell-O—sometimes as many as three boxes a day.

And the weight loss, my goodness! Every time I turn around, I'm running to the cobbler and asking him to punch another hole in my belt. At first, he was like, "On the house!" Then it was, "You again?"

I've gone down four notches and never feel hungry. More important, I never feel bitter, like I'm missing out. It's the Jell-O that allows me to eat my beloved hot dogs, which, calorie-wise, are pretty bad, though I blame a lot of that on the buns.

Amy says, "Do without them!"

Eating ground-up cow parts, though—the throat and udders and heart and uterus—alone on a plate without heavily processed white bread—that's just . . . gross.

HOLD THE HONEY

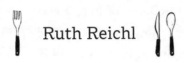

Ruth Reichl

Y FATHER ONCE BUILT A HOUSE ON THE EDGE OF A dark, forbidding, and wonderfully mysterious forest. For years I lacked the courage to venture into those woods. But the summer I was eight, my best friend, Jeanie, dared me to do it. "I'll come with you," she promised.

Holding hands, we took a few tentative steps, and then a few more, until we were deep in the forest, where the trees were so tall they blocked the sun and the only sounds were the singing birds and whispering wind. Suddenly we came upon the wreck of an ancient car. It was a Model T Ford, its engine rusted to a deep and resonant orange. Plants had taken root in the upholstery and burst through the roof. How did the car get there? Did a road once run through these woods? We could not have been more enchanted had we suddenly come upon a zebra or a lion.

We told no one about our discovery. But we went into the woods every day, seeking out buried treasure. Each time, we discovered something new: broken jars, old buttons, a book whose pages had absorbed so much rain, they'd turned into puffy little pillows. One day we found a china doll with a broken nose. Another, a leather change purse filled with coins covered in strange foreign symbols. The day we found an empty perfume bottle, we sniffed and sniffed until we were able to imagine the ghostly aroma of just-cut grass. We tried to re-create it, but making perfume, it turns out, is not child's play.

It was late in August when we unearthed a large round metal tin buried near the car. Prying it open, we found the remains of a cake. How long had it been there? We looked at each other. We shrugged. We were eight years old. We stuffed it into our mouths.

"Honey cake!" I cried, taking another bite. We sat on the damp ground, eating that cake, bite by bite. In my memory it was sweet and slightly nutty, with a tinge of vanilla and a hint of orange. It tasted like flowers and candy, like all the good things on Earth rolled into one. It was the most delicious thing I had ever eaten.

But the next day, when we went back, the car had vanished. So had all the buried treasures. We looked and looked, but we never found another trace. It was as if that old jalopy had been a figment of our imaginations. How could it have simply disappeared?

"It was the cake," said Jeanie. "We weren't supposed to eat it. I'm never eating honey again."

"Me either," I vowed.

Over the years I have eaten just about everything that's come my way. In Laos I happily consumed tea made of silkworm larva excrement while my friends looked on in horror. I drank rattlesnake blood in China. I've gobbled ant eggs on two continents. I consider guinea pig delicious and fermented squid guts even better. Yet I have never taken another bite of honey.

It's been a long time since I've seen Jeanie, but I'm willing to bet that she hasn't either.

Magic Cookies

These cookies always remind me of that summer in the forest. It is almost impossible to believe that a few ordinary ingredients can produce something so crisp, elegant, and mysteriously nutty. They do not, of course, contain a single drop of honey.

> 2½ cups rolled oats
> 1 cup dark brown sugar, packed
> 1 teaspoon baking powder
> 1 stick unsalted butter, melted
> 1 egg, beaten
> 1 teaspoon vanilla

Preheat the oven to 350°F.

Grease a large cookie sheet.

In a large bowl, mix the oats, brown sugar, and baking powder. Stir in the melted butter, the egg, and the vanilla.

Drop by small spoonfuls onto the cookie sheet and flatten with the back of a spoon.

Bake for about 8 to 10 minutes, or until the edges of the cookies begin to brown.

Remove the baking sheet from the oven and allow it to sit for a couple of minutes before removing the cookies.

If they stick, return the sheet to the oven for a minute.

PLUM PUDDING CHRISTMAS

 Zosia Mamet

I HAVE A PLETHORA OF VIVID AND FULLY FLESHED MEMORIES of my first five years of life. But we moved from Cambridge, Massachusetts, to Los Angeles when I was five. After that, it's odd—a wasteland, memories sporadic and few and far between. And they are either ones of true joy or utter horror.

I hated Los Angeles. I felt like I was stuck inside of some sort of sick loop. A continuous seventy-degrees and sunny Groundhog Day, equally as torturous as the day before. My new school in L.A. was a Christian prep school where our uniform skirts were made out of the same material they make dog leashes from. I started there in first grade, and until the day I left, a week into my seventh-grade year, I was bullied aggressively and relentlessly by the forty-one other children in my class. And we're not talking teasing or run-of-the-mill bullying. As a united front my classmates tortured me daily with tactics spanning from mind games to physical attacks. I still have a small black scar on the inside of my right knee where a male classmate stabbed me with a pencil as I walked past his desk, for no reason. And I was always blamed for whatever had happened. My classmates would band together and twist the situation to be my fault. I was constantly in the principal's office being reprimanded for misconduct I did not commit. Every morning when we got to school, I'd have to be physically pried from the front seat of our car as I screamed, "Please don't make me go!" School was a *Twilight Zone*–esque living nightmare.

But there was an escape from this daily hell: Christmas break. Every year since I was born, my mother, my sister, and I would head to a small town in Massachusetts where my maternal grandmother lived. We also spent summers there.

I. FUCKING. LOVE. CHRISTMAS. Even now as an adult, I go *ham* on Christmas. I do all of the shopping and wrapping for both my family and my husband's, all of our friends, colleagues, anyone I can fathom. It warms my soul. I'd possibly even say it's my favorite time of year. The smells, the music, all of it. My best friends are convinced I was an elf in a previous life, and once Christmas rolls around, I disappear into full-blown "elf mode." The search for the perfect gift has forever been one of my favorite parts of Christmas. Finding something someone will truly cherish, that's what does it for me. And there is no question that this love of everything Christmas came from my maternal grandmother.

My grandmother *adored* Christmas. She made the holiday and the entire time surrounding it . . . I mean, *magical* doesn't even really do it justice. She would get a tree before we got there but always waited for me to decorate it with her. We did it together, just the two of us. As she took out each ornament, she would tell me the story behind it.

My grandmother loved tradition and history. She kept and treasured all things. And that's what these ornaments were—magical Christmas treasures. Every time we finished, we would stare at the tree with pride. The moment we turned on the lights was always one that gave me goose bumps. She also always had boxes of clementines (that I would eat and eat and eat until I felt ill), which filled the house with the smell of citrus, along with her signature holiday scent: cloves in water on the stove. Bing Crosby and the like playing in the background.

And traditions, endless traditions, existed within my family. There were ones leading up to Christmas Eve, like decorating this male nude statue made by a famous sculptor friend of my grandmother's. The sculpture lived on the mantel above the fireplace, and throughout the week leading up to Christmas it was everyone's job to decorate him. We'd add little things, like ribbon my grandmother saved tied in bows around his head. A skirt taped around his waist fashioned from an old Christmas-colored dish towel. An ornament, stolen from the tree, hanging from his hand. And on Christmas Eve, we'd photograph him so that that year's iteration of his "Christmas best" was memorialized.

Then there were gift-wrapping traditions. My grandmother saved every piece of wrapping paper that was remotely salvageable and had a *massive* box of it that she kept in her basement and would bring out every year as the time to wrap came. On Christmas morning she'd sit in her special chair waiting patiently as we tore open presents, flinging wrapping paper into the air. As soon as it hit the floor, she'd snatch it up and sit on her throne, gingerly running her hand over the discarded paper, trying to smooth it out, fold it up, and save it for the following year. The funny thing is, I don't think we ever reused a single piece of that saved paper. But she saved it just the same.

And then, of course, there was Christmas Eve. We'd carol after din-ner, always in the snow or freezing cold, after which we'd return home to my grandmother's house for hot cocoa before we went to midnight mass at the three-hundred-year-old church in town. I wasn't raised re-ligiously, but I always found such magic at those midnight masses. The dimmed lights, everyone singing Christmas hymns holding candles, the church covered in garlands, and the scent of pine surrounding the room like a protective layer, holding us, hugging us, keeping the magic in.

Then we'd head home. Each of the children was allowed to open one present before bed. After, I would *fight* with every ounce of my being to try to stay awake. To maybe, just maybe, hear the reindeers' hooves on the roof or Santa munching on a cookie in the living room. All of the lights in the house off except for the twinkling glow of the tree, which filled the home with indescribable magic. The kind you know is there but can never explain or touch. I believed in Santa Claus for probably much too long. But, like I said, my real life was basically a repeat of the worst Monday of your life, so I held on to any form of escapism I could. And Santa Claus was that in spades. My grandmother knew that.

Christmas morning was, without fail, an explosion of magic and joy. Presents that to this day I don't know where they could have been hidden because I searched, trust me, I fucking *searched*, were strewn about the living room. Traditional Christmas morning pancakes were eaten and consumed between ripping open our gifts and showing off those we were most proud of.

Once the living room finally resembled the fallout of wrapping-paper warfare, everyone then dispersed to play with their new toys, and my grandmother headed for the kitchen to make Christmas dinner. The dinner was *filled* with family traditions. Poppers with horrible gifts. Paper crowns that nobody was ever allowed to take off, even if yours broke (which they almost always did). And the food, always the same food. The classics, of course: sweet potatoes with marshmallows (which I know is a point of contention for lots of folks, but as a small child I loved them). Stuffing filled with all the bells and whistles, mashed potatoes with gravy, so much gravy (I swear my grandmother would make a vat of it). Cranberry sauce made from scratch *and* out of the can to make everyone happy (I know this is a hot topic and can be very triggering for some during the holidays . . . I believe the divide between the kind of cranberry sauce you like has ruined many a family holiday dinner). And always a turkey to end all turkeys. I remember constantly being perplexed at how *that* turkey fit in my grandmother's oven as a child. It was too big. It couldn't have. . . . But again, it was just another part of the Christmas magic.

And then, of course, there was dessert. Pumpkin pie, pecan pie, Christmas cookies . . . *but* the biggest part of the meal was the plum pudding. Legend has it that this recipe traveled over with my ancestors from Scotland on some ship a long, long, long time ago. My grandmother had the recipe handwritten on a note card kept in her recipe box. The card was worn and stained with who knows what from all the plum puddings made in the past. For some reason (I don't understand science), the pudding is made about a month out in a mold and has to set. And that's something else I always loved and appreciated: that my grandmother, weeks and months before Christmas music had even begun to play in stores, was preparing for our traditional Christmas meal by making the pièce de résistance, the plum pudding.

Once it was time for dessert, the classic pies would come out, and then, of course, the plum pudding would be revealed. It would be doused with some sort of liquor . . . my guess today is most likely a type of bourbon. And then it would be one lucky person's job to light it on fire. Watching that cake be lit on fire never failed to excite me. Then my grandmother would drench the pudding in something she called "foamy sauce," which I'm pretty sure was just eggs and sugar whipped together. We'd all dig in. It's hard to describe the taste. It's not a complex dessert, but the flavor isn't subtle either. And it's not something you'd expect a child to like, but I FUCKING LOVED IT. It was rich and sweet, but the hint of liquor gave it a slight kick while the foamy sauce added a sugary, thick creaminess that rounded the entire thing out. I remember always searching for the perfect bite—the ratio of plum pudding to foamy sauce just right, creating an explosion of Christmas flavor in my mouth.

Once the pudding was finished, a bit of a sadness would set in. Because it signified the end. I knew we'd stay only for a bit longer at my grandmother's and then it would be time to return to Los Angeles and my own personal hellhole—that military-like Christian school in Pacific Palisades, those evil young girls who lived to make me miserable . . .

When the plane touched down in L.A., I would try to muster every ounce of the Christmas magic I had just experienced and put it in a box deep inside of me. And I'd use it for as long as I could to get through another year until I was able to escape the bullying again. When I could escape back to my grandmother's house up on a hill filled with Christmas magic.

I don't know if I could have gotten through that period without that escape, without that magic, without that reprieve. It saved me. It gave me hope. And it healed me. Those two weeks would fill me up with enough joy to hold my breath until I could get back there again. And to this day I know that's why I cherish Christmas so deeply. I will forever be so deeply grateful to my grandmother. To her love of Christmas and tradition, to her commitment to making this holiday magical to a degree that made the rest of the world fall away. My grandmother passed years ago. But I still imagine her every Christmas wherever she is prepping that plum pudding and getting ready to decorate the tree.

ACKNOWLEDGMENTS

By definition, this book was a team effort. It would not exist without each and every individual who gave themselves to it in one shape or form. First and foremost, I want to acknowledge the contributors. Their enthusiasm to write their essays, the exquisite words they shared, the vulnerability they all showed within their storytelling . . . This book is a quilt of their hearts and minds. I had hopes and dreams of what it could be, and they all made it better than I could have imagined. Thanks to all of them for adding to this literary potluck.

I am also indebted to my amazing editor, Meg Leder, and Penguin Books for believing in this wild idea and in me, and for holding my hand through the entire process. Meg, I could not have asked for a better editor or friend.

Thank you to my amazing book agent, Melissa Flashman, and my exceptional manager, Sally Ware, who also were instrumental in bringing this book into the world.

Yan Yu Lee, thank you for your magical illustrations. You completed this book by bringing it to life with your drawings.

Ann Volkwein, our recipe tester, thank you for making sure each and every recipe is as delicious as it's meant to be and is foolproof for all of our readers.

Jean Louise O'Sullivan, thank you for keeping everyone on task, every file, essay, contract, recipe, email correspondence, and everything else I cannot think of in order, on time, and on record. I could not have done this without you.

And last, but certainly not least, I would like to acknowledge my wonderful husband, Evan, who continued to encourage me to actually make this book. He gently nudged until I finally did something about it, and now, well, here we are. Thank you, Ev, for giving me the push I needed. I love you.

ABOUT THE CONTRIBUTORS

234 **Mari Andrew** is a writer and artist living in New York City. She is the author of two books, *Am I There Yet?* and *My Inner Sky.*

116 **Nikole Beckwith** is a playwright, writer, and filmmaker based in New York. She has made plays with The Public Theater, Playwrights Horizons, Clubbed Thumb, the National Theatre of London, and the Royal Court. Her films (*Stockholm, Pennsylvania* and *Together Together*) both premiered at the Sundance Film Festival in the U.S. Dramatic Competition. She was rejected from Juilliard four times.

134 **Jillian Bell** is an actor (*Brittany Runs a Marathon, Godmothered, 22 Jump Street*) who loves safe thrills (haunted houses, the Tower of Terror). In her spare time she swims, hangs with her dogs, and has panic attacks. Bell's family has been known to call her "dramatic" and "sensitive," but her favorite nickname is "Jilly." She thinks the score from *A Few Good Men* is "simple yet chilling."

15 **Andrew Bevan** is a writer and creative strategist who spent a decade at *Vogue* and *Teen Vogue* after cutting his teeth at Miramax and on *Charlie Rose*. He is known for having a keen eye for up-and-coming talent in entertainment and fashion, as well as regularly interviewing various cultural icons. His writing can be seen in *Vogue, Architectural Digest, Vogue Japan, 10 Magazine, Harper's Bazaar,* and *Midtempo*—a digital music zine he co-created. In addition, Bevan has done extensive creative storytelling content for a vast portfolio of luxury and main-stay fashion brands and starred in his own YouTube series, *Breakfast with Bevan*. He lives in downtown Manhattan with his dog, Walter.

126 Kathryn Budig is an internationally celebrated yoga teacher, author, storyteller, mythology buff, and mama to her two senior dogs. She is the author of *Aim True* and *The Women's Health Big Book of Yoga*, along with founding The Inky Phoenix book club and her online platform, Haus of Phoenix.

225 Michelle Buteau is the host of the popular Netflix competition series *The Circle* and is starring in her own scripted show for Netflix, *Survival of the Thick-est*, based on her autobiographical book of essays of the same name, published by Gallery Books. Other film and TV credits include *Marry Me*, *First Wives Club*, *Always Be My Maybe*, *Awkwafina Is Nora from Queens*, *Russian Doll*, and *Someone Great*. Buteau's one-hour comedy special *Michelle Buteau: Welcome to Buteaupia* is streaming on Netflix and recently won the Critics' Choice Award for Best Comedy Special.

110 Sian Clifford is an award-winning British actress. She is best known for her role as Claire in the multi-award-winning and critically acclaimed *Fleabag*, for which she won a BAFTA and was nominated for Emmy, SAG, and Critics' Choice awards. She is the founder of Still Space, an online platform dedicated to inspiring conscious living, for which she was named Hay House Publishing's and *Psychologies* magazine's New Wise Voice in 2016.

241 Sloane Crosley is an essayist and novelist based in New York City. She is the author of the essay collections *I Was Told There'd Be Cake*, *How Did You Get This Number*, and *Look Alive Out There*, as well as the novels *The Clasp* and *Cult Classic*. Her next book, *Grief Is for People*, will be published in 2023.

42 Whitney Cummings is a comedian, writer, podcaster, and horse-jewelry hoarder. She loves horses and dogs and people who love horses and dogs.

91 Kaley Cuoco is an actor, a producer, but most important, an animal lover.

4 Stephanie Danler is a novelist, memoirist, and screenwriter. She is the author of *Stray* and the international bestseller *Sweetbitter*. She is the creator and executive producer of the *Sweetbitter* television series on Starz. She is based in Los Angeles and is at work on a novel.

220 Ted Danson is an actor.

139 Garance Doré is a French author and illustrator, but she would love it if you called her an everyday philosopher. She is not exactly sure where she lives, but she is currently working on her second book while sharing her many exotic points of view about life in her world-famous newsletter. She is far too modest to share any of the awards she received but will gladly tell you all the details about her astonishing visit to a sex club. Her English is far from perfect, but don't worry, she's taking Latin. *Castigat ridendo mores.*

81 Beanie Feldstein is an actor, producer, and writer living in New York City. She's played Fanny Brice in the revival of *Funny Girl* on Broadway. She recently starred as Monica Lewinsky in *Impeachment: American Crime Story*, which she also produced. Her films include *Booksmart*, *Lady Bird*, and *How to Build a Girl*. She found her love of writing while studying sociology at Wesleyan University.

203 Matt Flanders is a TV and film writer and producer based in New York City. Most recently, he produced Tony Stone's *Ted K*, and he's currently working on Richard Press's *Farnsworth House*. Before starting his own production company, In Your Face Entertainment, he worked in production and development at Plan B Entertainment, assisting with films such as *Eat Pray Love*, *World War Z*, and *12 Years a Slave*. Flanders also writes for live events and awards shows for TV and spends his downtime on a farm in upstate New York with his husband and two dogs, Steak Frites and Whopper.

185 Naomi Fry is a staff writer at *The New Yorker*. She was born in Israel and now lives in Brooklyn with her family.

232 Tony Hale is an Emmy Award–winning actor known for his work on *Veep*, *Arrested Development*, *The Mysterious Benedict Society*, *Being the Ricardos*, and

Toy Story 4. He also co-wrote the book *Archibald's Next Big Thing*, which later became an animated show on Netflix and Peacock.

171   **Katie Holmes** is an actor and director. She loves reading poetry from the romantic period, watching old Cassavetes films, and spending time with her friends making art. She lives with her daughter in New York City.

146   **Silas Howard** started in filmmaking with his first feature *By Hook or by Crook* (Sundance, 2002), made with Harry Dodge. His credits include *Pose*, *Dickinson*, *Transparent*, *This Is Us*, *High Maintenance*, *Everything's Gonna Be Okay*, and his most recent feature, *A Kid Like Jake* (Sundance, 2018). He was a founding member of the seminal queer punk band Tribe 8 and co-founder of San Francisco's legendary café and performance space The Bearded Lady Truckstop and Coffee Shop.

72   **Sarah Jones** is a Tony-winning solo performer, writer, comedian, and filmmaker known for her multicultural character work, including her Broadway hit *Bridge & Tunnel*, originally produced by Meryl Streep, and the critically acclaimed show *Sell/Buy/Date*. Jones recently launched Foment Productions, a social justice–focused entertainment company. The hybrid documentary *Sell/Buy/Date* is its first production and Jones's directorial debut. She's from New York but now lives in Los Angeles, where she yearns daily for a good bagel.

130   **Daniel Lavery** is the author of *Something That May Shock and Discredit You*, *The Merry Spinster*, and *Texts from Jane Eyre*. He is the co-founder of The Toast and the proprietor of *The Chatner* newsletter, and formerly the Dear Prudence advice columnist at *Slate*.

188   A multifaceted creator, **John Leguizamo** has established a career that defies categorization. With boundless energy and creativity, his work in film, theater, television, and literature covers a variety of genres, continually threatening to create a few of its own. Leguizamo received a Special Tony Award at the 2018 Tony Awards after wrapping an extended Broadway run of *Latin History for Morons*, his latest one-man show, delivering his take on five hundred years of Latin history spanning the Aztec and Incan empires to World War II. Leguizamo's *Ghetto Klown*, a graphic novel adaptation of his Broadway one-man show of the same name, was nominated for an Eisner Award. He also released a comic book, *Freak*, based on his solo show of the same name. Recently, Leguizamo earned both Critics' Choice and Emmy award nominations for his role as Raymond Santana Sr. in the Netflix series *When They See Us*, and an Emmy nomination for his role in the Paramount Network television series *Waco* alongside Taylor Kitsch and Michael Shannon. His directorial debut, *Critical Thinking*, was selected to premiere at SXSW Film Festival. Leguizamo has garnered numerous other accolades throughout his career, including an Emmy Award and a Drama Desk Award, as well as nominations for Tony Awards and Golden Globes. Leguizamo's film credits include, but are not limited to, *Carlito's Way*, *To Wong Foo, Thanks for Everything! Julie Newmar*, *Romeo + Juliet*, *The Pest*, *Moulin Rouge!*, *Summer of Sam*, *The Lincoln Lawyer*, and the *Ice Age* franchise. He currently resides in New York City with his wife and two children.

64 **Hamish Linklater** is an actor and writer. His plays include *The Vandal*, *The Cheats*, and *The Whirligig*. He grew up, an only child of a single mom, at Shakespeare & Company in Lenox, Massachusetts. Now he lives in Los Angeles, California, with his partner, Lily, three daughters, a son, and a rescue dog named Bruce.

198 **Anita Lo** is a Michelin-starred chef, a cookbook author, and a knight of the Order of Agricultural Merit of France, and is based in New York City. She currently hosts culinary tours around the planet with a travel company called Tour de Forks.

12 Award-winning actress-singer **Patti LuPone**, when not at work on Broadway or the West End Stage or in front of a camera, likes nothing more than to go digging for clams and other crustaceans on the nearest sandbar.

142 **Kavi Ahuja Moltz** is the co-founder and designer of D.S. & DURGA. She is a New Yorker who loves to throw dinner parties, go to the beach, get tattoos, drink martinis, read Russian books, take walks, and hang out with her husband and two children.

59   Alaina Moore is a songwriter, producer, and primary artist in the band Tennis. She received her philosophy degree from the University of Colorado, and is co-founder of the label Mutually Detrimental along with her husband and bandmate, Patrick Riley. When she is not touring the world with her band, she is off-shore sailing, and has logged more than ten thousand ocean miles.

196   Lamorne Morris was tapped as the lead of the hybrid live-action/animated Hulu series *Woke*, inspired by the life and art of cartoonist Keith Knight. Morris appeared in the Netflix comedy film *Desperados* alongside Anna Camp, Robbie Amell, Nasim Pedrad, and Heather Graham; it debuted in July 2020. He was also in Sony's *Bloodshot* opposite Vin Diesel, as well as in *How It Ends*, which was released in 2021. Additionally, Morris was seen in *National Geographic*'s limited series *Valley of the Boom*, opposite Bradley Whitford and Steve Zahn. He is best known for playing fan favorite "Winston" on Fox's popular comedy *New Girl* for seven seasons, where he starred opposite Zooey Deschanel, Max Greenfield, and Jake Johnson. His additional past projects include the Warner Bros. film *Game Night*, with Jason Bateman and Rachel McAdams; the Netflix film *Sandy Wexler*, where he starred opposite Adam Sandler; and the hilarious *Barbershop: The Next Cut*, starring opposite Ice Cube.

121   Kwame Onwuachi is a James Beard Award–winning chef and co-author of the critically acclaimed memoir *Notes from a Young Black Chef*, which is being turned into a feature film by A24. Onwuachi's résumé is incomparable: He has been named one of *Food & Wine*'s Best New Chefs, *Esquire* magazine's 2019 Chef of the Year, and is a 30 Under 30 honoree by both Zagat and *Forbes*. He's also been featured in *Time*'s 100 Next list and has been named the most important chef in America by the *San Francisco Chronicle*. Onwuachi appeared as a judge on season 18 of *Top Chef* in April 2021. He first appeared as a contestant on the show in season 13. He also was the host of the 2021 James Beard Awards in Chicago. Onwuachi currently serves as *Food & Wine*'s executive producer. In this newly appointed role, he will collaborate on big brand moments and events, including the Food & Wine Classic in Aspen. He is also the creator of The Family Reunion: Presented by Kwame Onwuachi, an annual multiday event taking place in Middleburg, Virginia, that celebrates diversity in the hospitality community.

84 **Rosie Perez** is an activist, producer, two-time Emmy-nominated choreographer, and Emmy-nominated and Oscar-nominated actress. Perez is known for roles in such films as *Fearless, Do the Right Thing, White Men Can't Jump,* and *Pineapple Express,* among many others. She has been an activist for many causes. In 2010, President Barack Obama appointed her to the Presidential Advisory Council on HIV/AIDS (PACHA). Perez is the author of *Handbook for an Unpredictable Life: How I Survived Sister Renata and My Crazy Mother, and Still Came Out Smiling (with Great Hair).*

94 **Busy Philipps** is a human being who has given birth twice. She has done many things in her life, mostly in the field of entertainment, with varying degrees of success. She has written one book, *This Will Only Hurt a Little,* which was a *New York Times* bestseller even though it wasn't sold in airports! She enjoys watching Norwegian teen shows with her teenager, Birdie, and losing board games to her younger child, Cricket.

39 **Andrew Rannells** is originally from Omaha, Nebraska. As a child, he was a respected altar boy. As an adult, he is best known for dancing and cursing on Broadway in *The Book of Mormon* and taking his clothes off in HBO's *Girls.*

259 **Ruth Reichl** has been writing about food since 1971. She has been a chef, a restaurant owner, a restaurant critic for the *Los Angeles Times* and *The New York Times,* the editor in chief of *Gourmet,* the book editor of the Modern Library Food series, and the author of six memoirs and a novel and the editor of *The Gourmet Cookbook*—which have all been *New York Times* bestsellers.

47 Actress, singer, and activist **Michaela Jaé Rodriguez** is known for her work as the housemother, Blanca, in the third and final season of Ryan Murphy's groundbreaking series *Pose* on FX. Her work on the series earned her a historical Emmy nomination for Outstanding Lead Actress in a Drama Series and won her a Golden Globe Award. In June 2021, she released her debut single, "Something to Say," via Access Records.

104 **Jess Rona** is the most influential dog groomer today, having built a cult-like following on social media with her signature musical slow-mo blowout videos and her impressive celebrity pet clientele. As a skilled groomer, director, and comedian, Rona has created a multidimensional grooming empire. She is the executive producer and star of the most adorable competition series of all time: *Haute Dog* on HBO Max, inspired by her life and brand. When she's not creating poodle content, you can find her at her adorably unique brick-and-mortar flagship in Larchmont Village in Los Angeles or snuggling with her husband, actor Eric Edelstein, and their two rescue mutts, Meemu and Chupie.

175   **Jordan Roth** is a self-expression evangelist, couture devotee, and the-aterista. As president of Jujamcyn Theaters, he championed some of the most influential and successful shows on Broadway, including *Moulin Rouge! The Musical, Hadestown, Kinky Boots, Springsteen on Broadway*, and *The Book of Mormon*. A five-time Tony Award winner, Roth produced the Tony Award–winning revival of *Angels in America*, and the Pulitzer Prize– and Tony Award for Best Play–winning *Clybourne Park*.

209   **Danny Sangra** studied graphic design at Central Saint Martins and has since become a multidisciplinary artist who works across platforms, including illustration, writing, and film. As an illustrator, he has worked with and collaborated with brands such as Burberry, Hermès, and Nike. As a filmmaker Sangra has created films for Adidas, Balenciaga, Miu Miu, and Mercedes-Benz. A polymath of creativity, Sangra's artwork is recognizable through its use of multimedia collages of appropriated mass media with hand-drawn illustrations. His pieces are populated with word play and indiscreet streams of consciousness and commentary.

33   **Heidi Schreck** is a writer/performer living in Brooklyn with her partner, Kip Fagan, and their awesome twin daughters. Her latest play, *What the Constitution Means to Me*, was a finalist for the Pulitzer Prize and played an extended run on Broadway before touring the country.

254   **David Sedaris** is the author of thirteen books, including, most recently, *Happy-Go-Lucky, A Carnival of Snackery, The Best of Me*, and *Calypso*. He is a regular contributor to *The New Yorker* and BBC Radio 4. In 2019, he was inducted into the American Academy of Arts and Letters. He is a recipient of the Thurber Prize for American Humor, the Jonathan Swift Prize for Satire and Humor, and the Terry Southern Prize for Humor.

179   Leanne Shapton is a Canadian author, artist, and publisher based in New York City. Her latest book, *Guestbook*, is a collection of stories, and she is currently the art editor at *The New York Review of Books*. Shapton's *Swimming Studies* won the 2012 National Book Critics Circle Award for autobiography. Shapton is a fellow of the Royal Canadian Geographical Society and the co-founder of J&L Books.

49   Richard Shepard is an Emmy Award–winning director and writer whose feature films include the Golden Globe–nominated *The Matador*, starring Pierce Brosnan and Greg Kinnear; *Dom Hemingway*, starring Jude Law and Richard E. Grant; and *The Perfection*, starring Allison Williams and Logan Browning. Shepard has directed ten television pilots to pickup, including *Criminal Minds*, *Ugly Betty*, and *Zoey's Extraordinary Playlist*. Among his other projects, Shepard has directed twelve episodes of the HBO series *Girls*; several episodes of *The Handmaid's Tale*; the HBO short film *Tokyo Project*, starring Elisabeth Moss; as well as the Emmy-nominated HBO documentary *I Knew It Was You: Rediscovering John Cazale*.

154   Gabourey Sidibe is an award-winning actress, director, producer, voice artist, and author. Best known for her role in Lee Daniels's Academy Award–nominated film *Precious*, Sidibe's other film and television credits include *Tower Heist*, *Seven Psychopaths*, *Empire*, and *American Horror Story*. She's written a memoir called *This Is Just My Face: Try Not to Stare*, and will soon be directing the upcoming narrative feature *Pale Horse*.

246   Tulica Singh is a writer/director based in L.A. Her Vimeo staff-picked series *Croissant Man* (about an existential croissant) was one of the first independent web series to be distributed through Amazon Prime. With her feature film *Curses!*, she was chosen for the 2021 Sundance Screenwriters fellowship and a Comedy Central grant. She is dedicated to writing projects that blend satire with sincerity, but spends most of her time looking for her keys.

1   Patti Smith is a writer, performer, and recording and visual artist. Since 1975, Smith has recorded thirteen albums, including the seminal *Horses*. Her most popular song, the anthem "People Have the Power," was co-written with her late husband, Fred "Sonic" Smith. The couple had two children, Jackson and Jesse Paris. Smith was awarded the prestigious 2010 National Book Award for her bestselling memoir, *Just Kids,* chronicling her collaborative relationship with the artist Robert Mapplethorpe. Her books include *Woolgathering, M Train,* and *Year of the Monkey.* Smith holds the honor of Commandeur des Arts et des Lettres from the French Ministry of Culture. In 2007, she was inducted into the Rock & Roll Hall of Fame. In 2016, she was awarded the Burke Medal for Outstanding Contribution to Discourse through the Arts from Trinity College Dublin.

230 **Mark D. Sylvester** is the managing director of Philadelphia's Walnut Street Theatre, America's oldest theater. Over the past four decades, he has been associated with more than 450 theatrical productions, from summer stock to Broadway to regional theaters. An avid collector of musical theater recordings, his collection contains more than 3,000 cast albums from around the world. He co-authored the book *Walnut Street Theatre.*

214 **Jia Tolentino** is a staff writer at *The New Yorker* and the author of the bestselling essay collection *Trick Mirror,* which has been translated into eleven languages.

193 After noticing a lack of functional yet stylish laptop cases while working as a journalist for French TV, **Clare Vivier** decided to create her own line of handbags and accessories. Since 2008, Vivier has cultivated an identifiable aesthetic all her own, recognized worldwide as a style influencer with hundreds of thousands of followers across social media. After more than a decade, the Clare V. brand has grown to include eleven physical retail locations, more than one hundred wholesale partners around the globe, and a robust e-commerce business.

166 **iO Tillett Wright** is awful at telling people what he does. He is a writer, podcast host, producer, and is now making television. He has been an actor, a photographer, a publisher, a reporter, and is a lifelong activist. He is an amateur chef, clearly.

CREDITS

CREDITS